I0471878

Studies in Mixed Media

Figure and portraits by Benjamin Long, February 2012

Charmed Actresses

Studies of various faces and human designs over a period of times. Included is various paintings, sketches paintings of celebrities, historical figures and other designs that fit the description. All depictions described in this portfolio are the property of the artist, unless the work is work for hire then the rightful owner of the piece will be described in the description.

This is an illustration of the Cast of the Television Series Charmed. It features Holly Marie Combs, Alyssa Milano, as well as Rose McGowan.

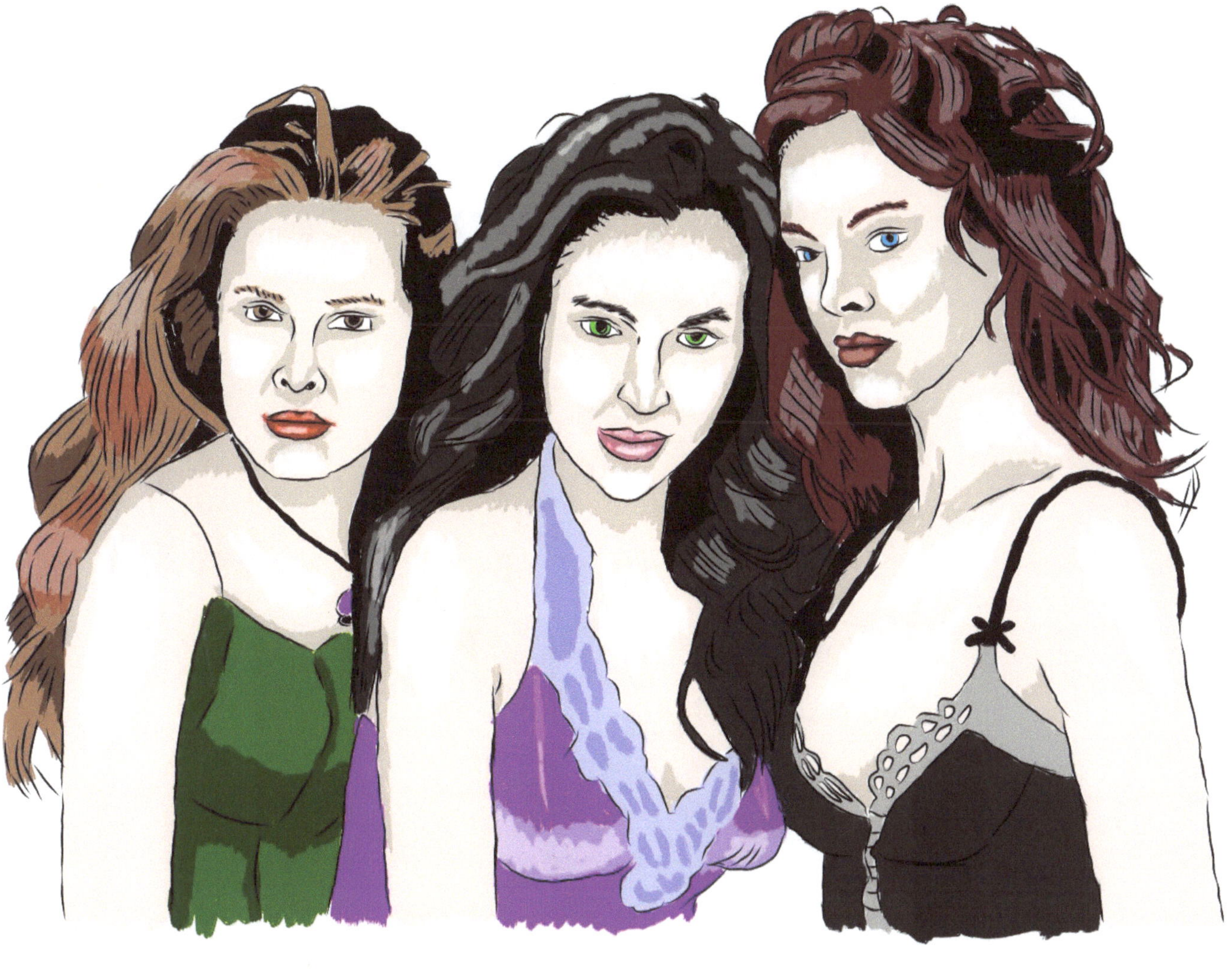

Free Gaza
Pelikan/ Digital

This is an Illustration of a Palestinian Protestor
being gunned down by Israeli forces.

"Free Gaza"
Benjamin Long
Copyright 2012 All Rights Reserved

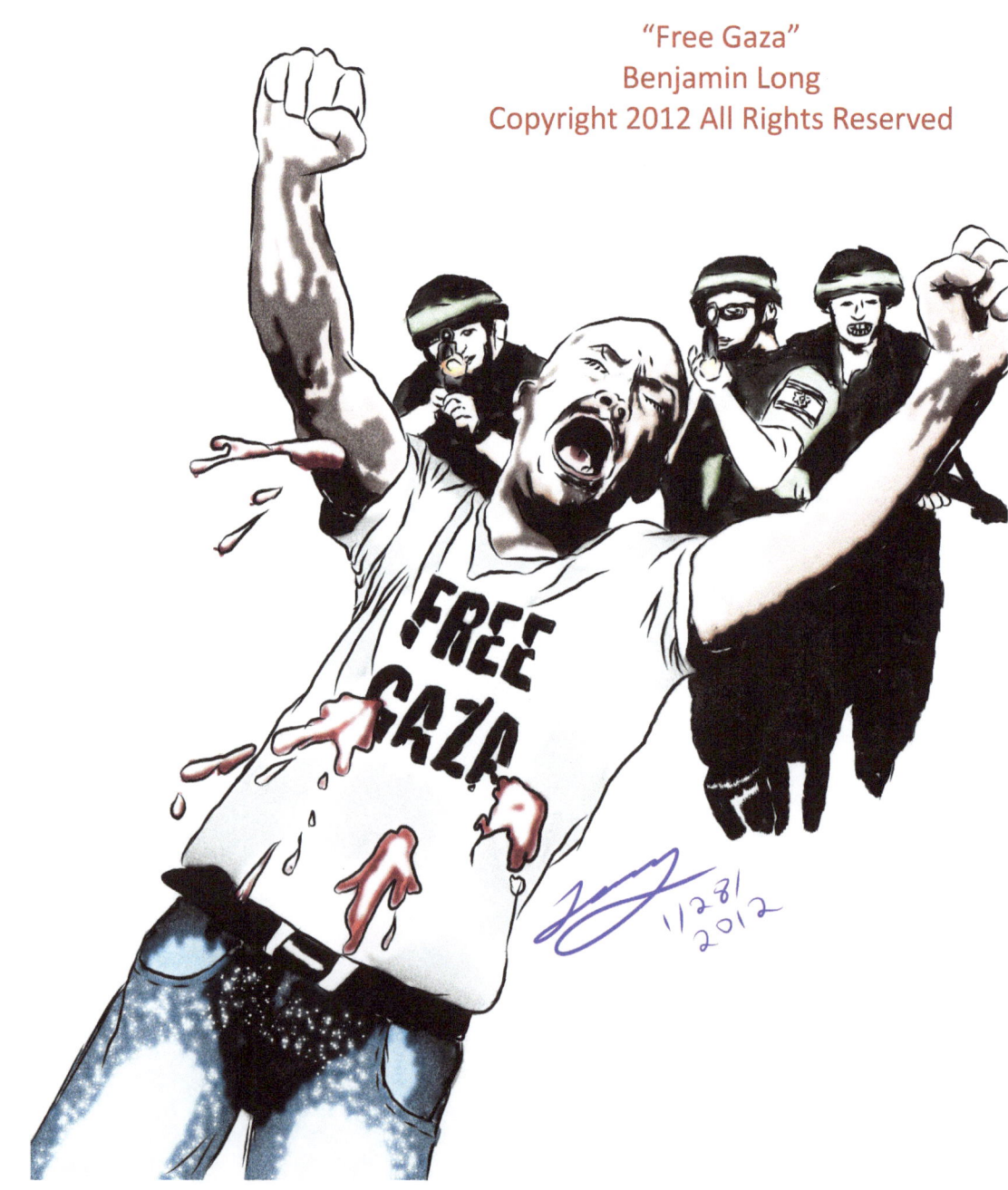

Sibling Rivalry
Comic/Pelikan

This is an Illustration of a pair of sibling Leopard Cubs that I illustrated. I found that it would be refreshing to put a humorous angle to the depiction.

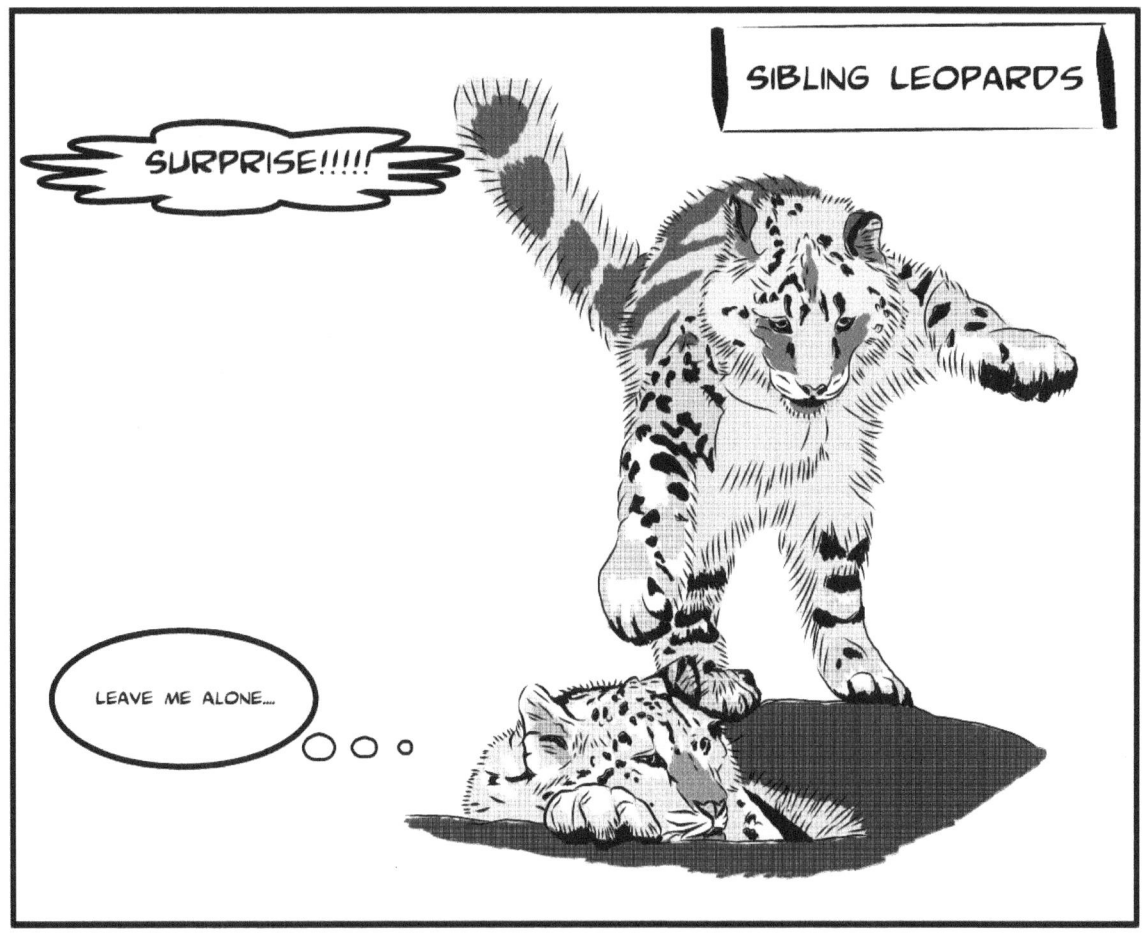

ILLUSTRATED BY BENJAMN LONG ALL RIGHTS RESERVED 2012

Old Woman

Pelikan Black 4001

Illustration of an Old Woman done as a Commission.

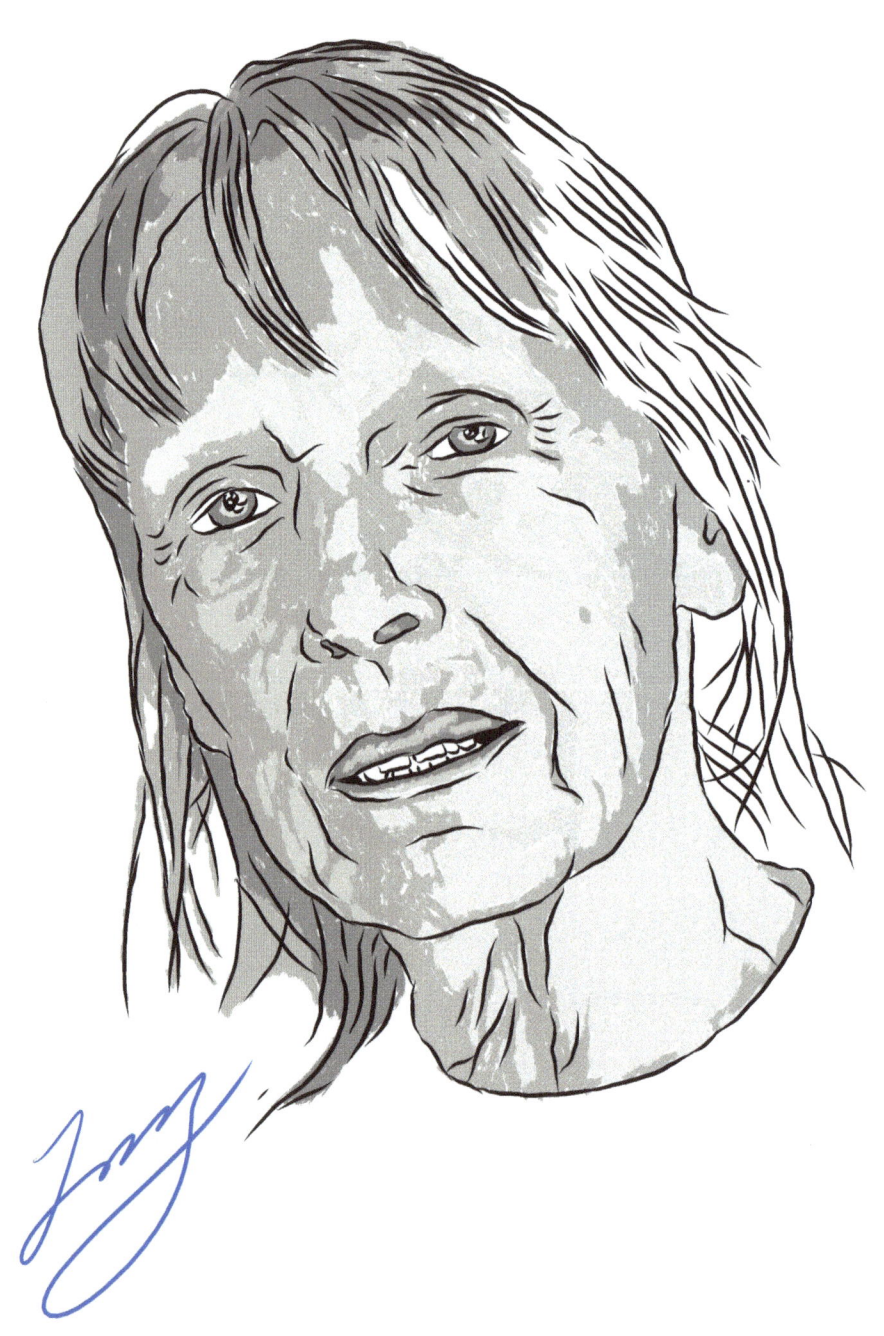

Resident Evil

Pelikan

Illustration of the Cast to the Resident Evil Movie. Illustrated are Milla Jovovich, and Michelle Rodriguez as well as the Actor that played Matt.

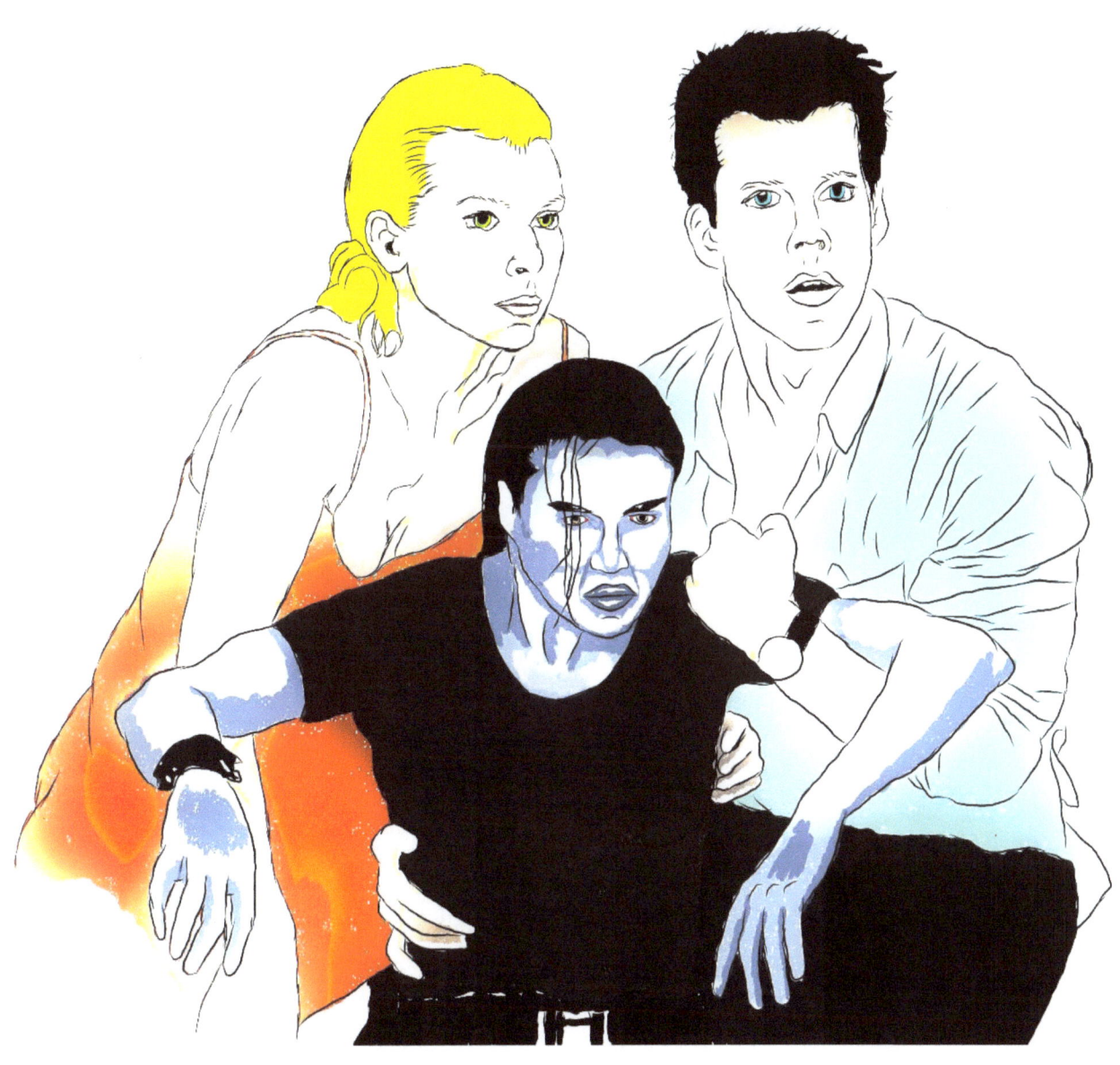

Super Natural

Acrylic Paint/Pelikan Ink

Illustration of Sam and Dean Winchester from the Television Series Supernatural

"Supernatural"
Benjamin Long
Copyright 2012 All Rights Reserved

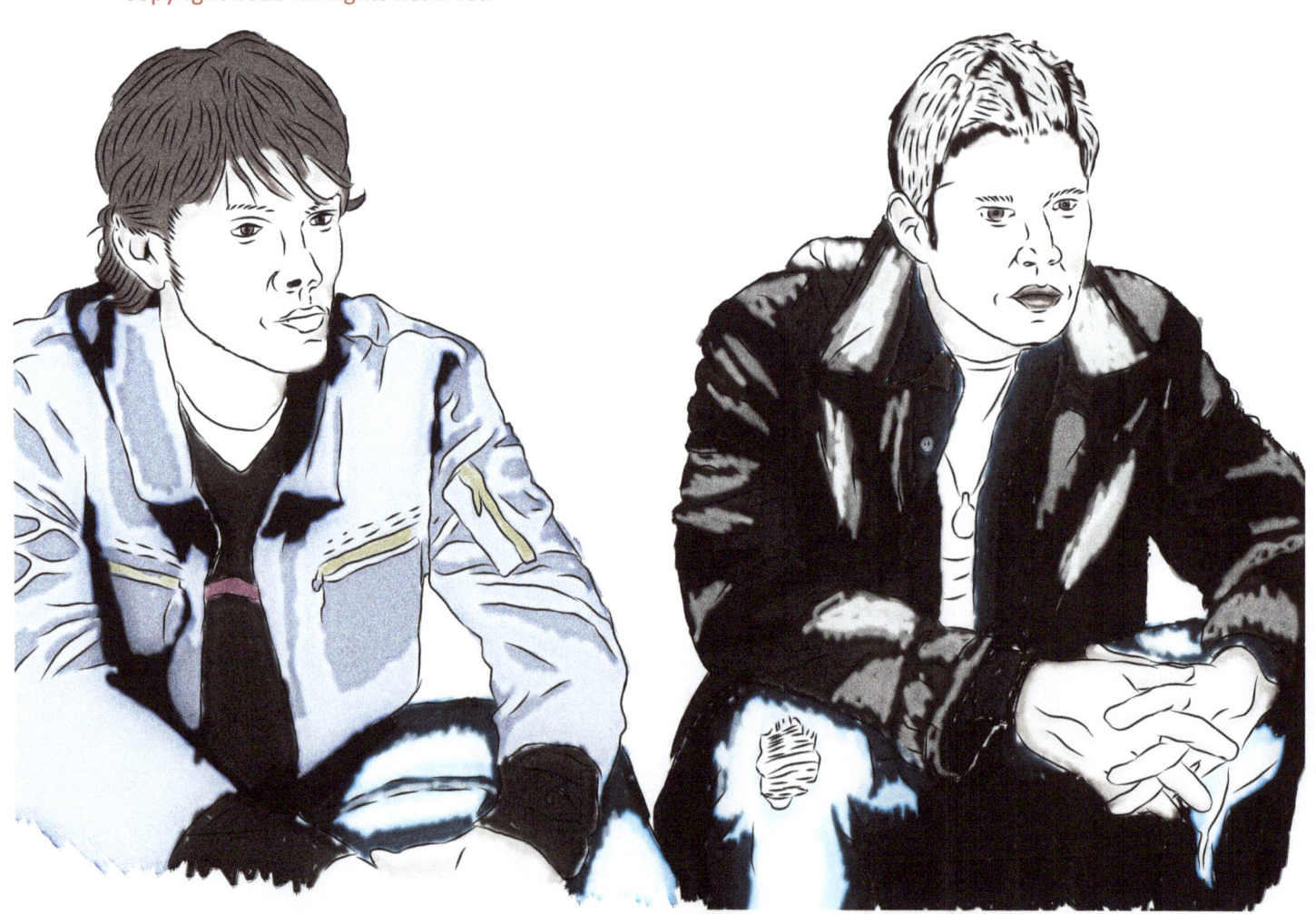

Sell Your Soul

Acrylic Paint/Pelikan Ink

Political Illustration regarding the US and Zionism.

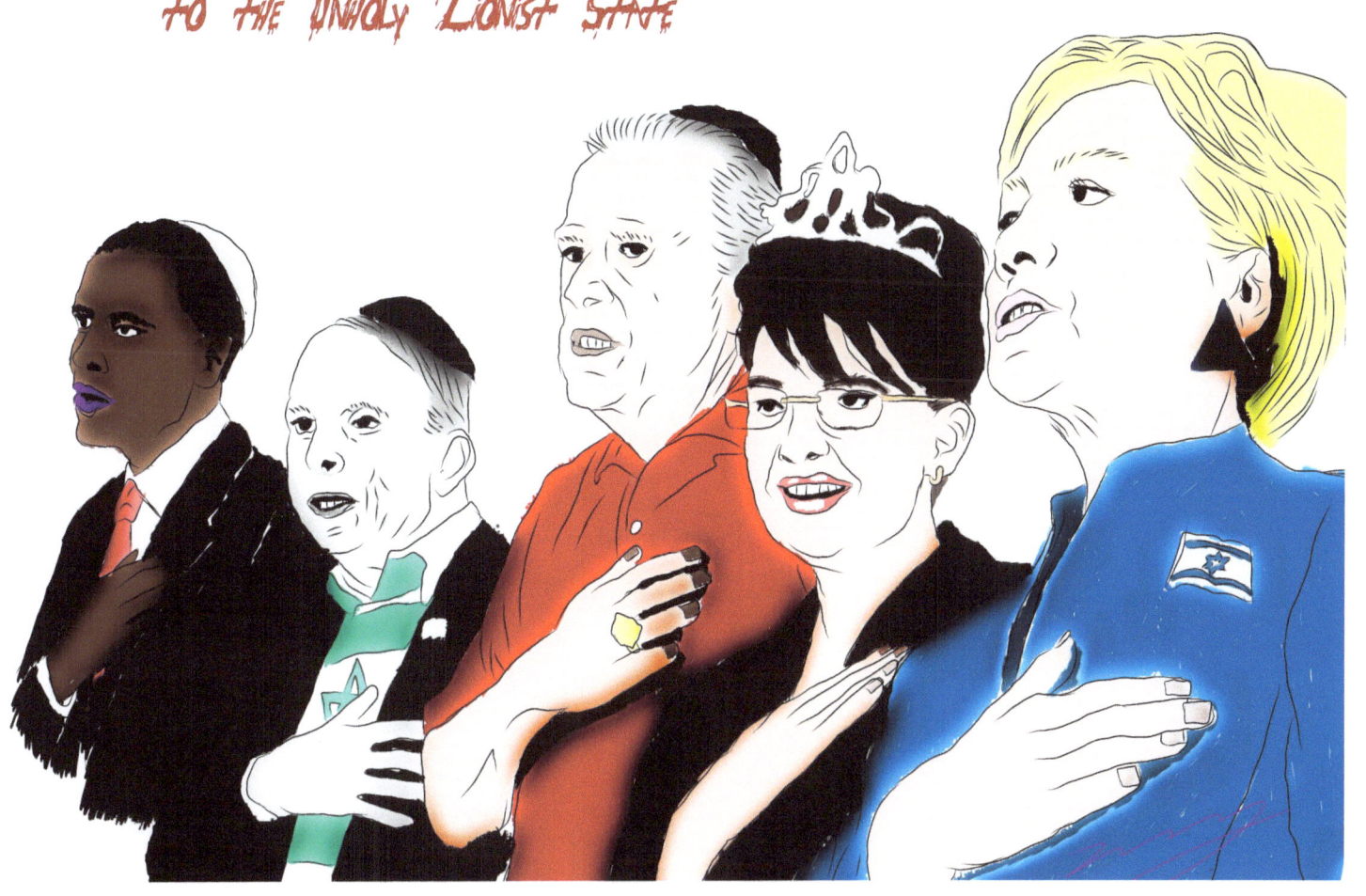

SELL YOUR SOUL
AND SWEAR ALLEGIANCE
TO THE UNHOLY ZIONIST STATE

Blonde Woman

Acrylic Paint/Pelikan Ink

Illustration of a Blonde haired Woman.

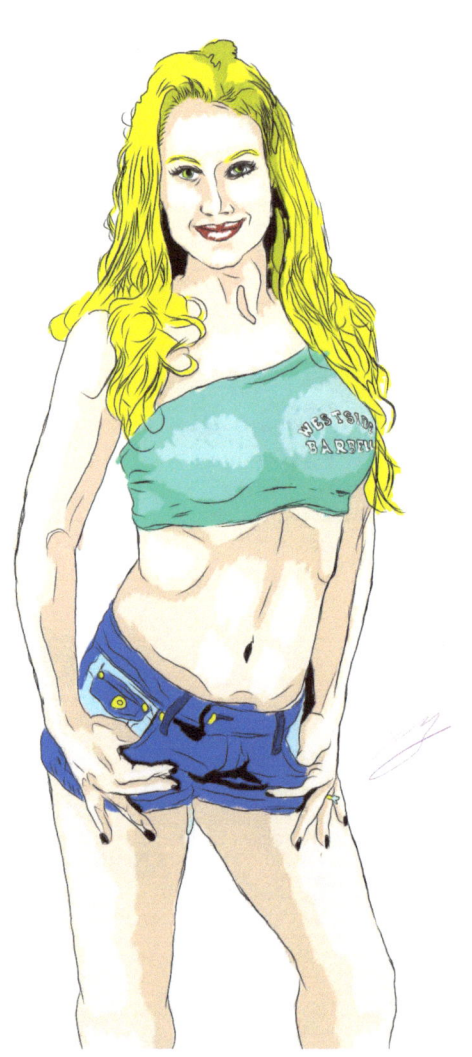
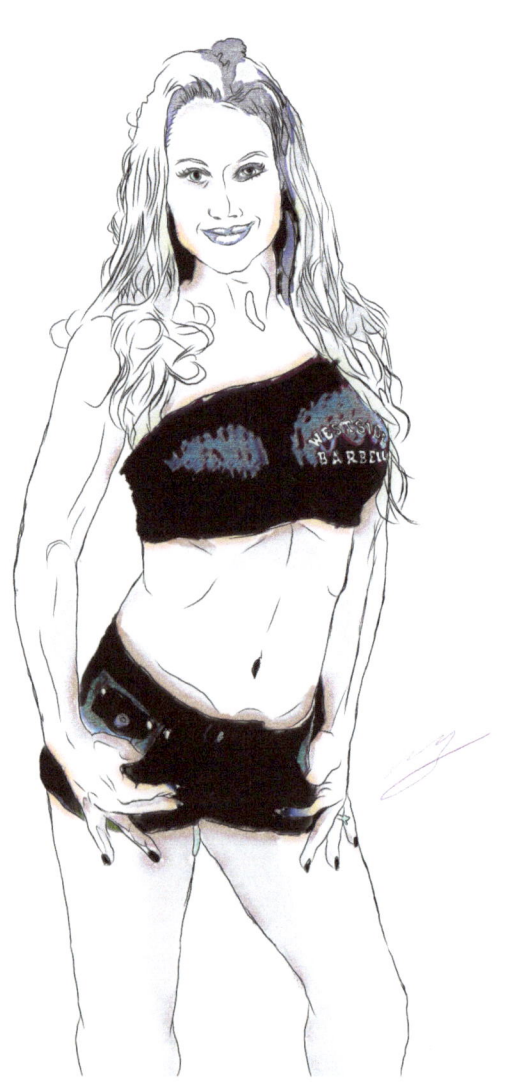

Import Pin Up

Acrylic Paint/Pelikan Ink

Illustration of a Foreign Car with a
Woman sitting on the Vehicle.

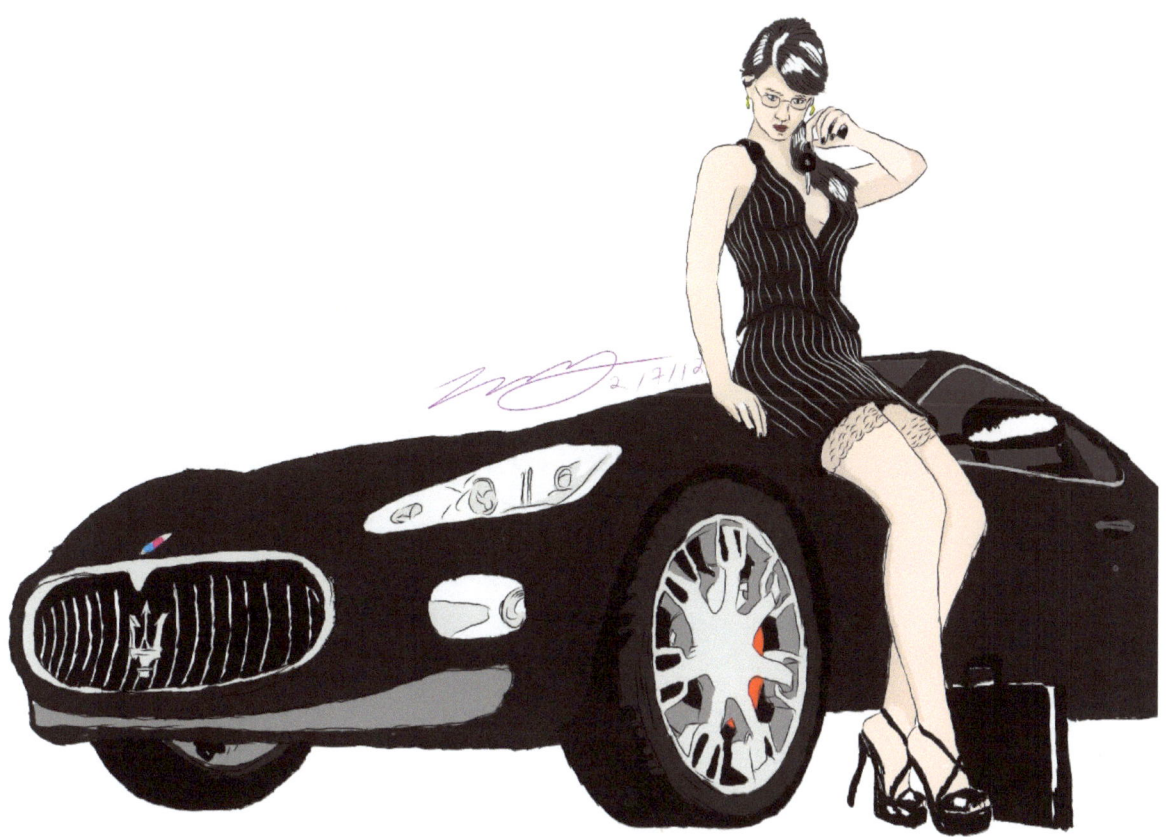

Corvette Z06

Colored Pencil/Pelikan Ink

Illustration of one of the fastest cars in the world. I believe this was the pace car for the Daytona races.

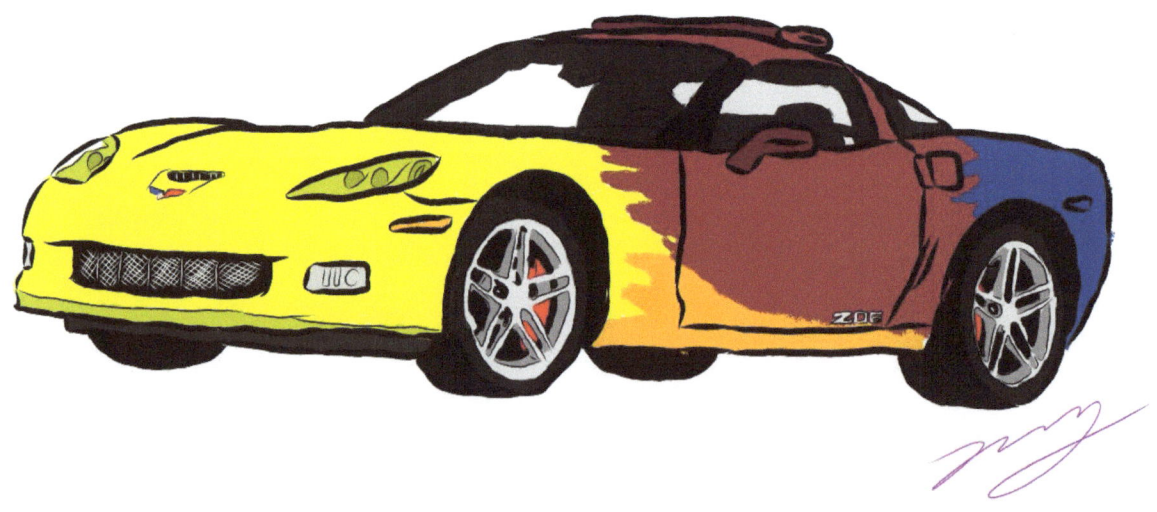

Kaley Cuoco Pin Up

Digital Painting

Digital rendering of Kaley Cuoco in front of a 99 Pontiac Grand Prix.

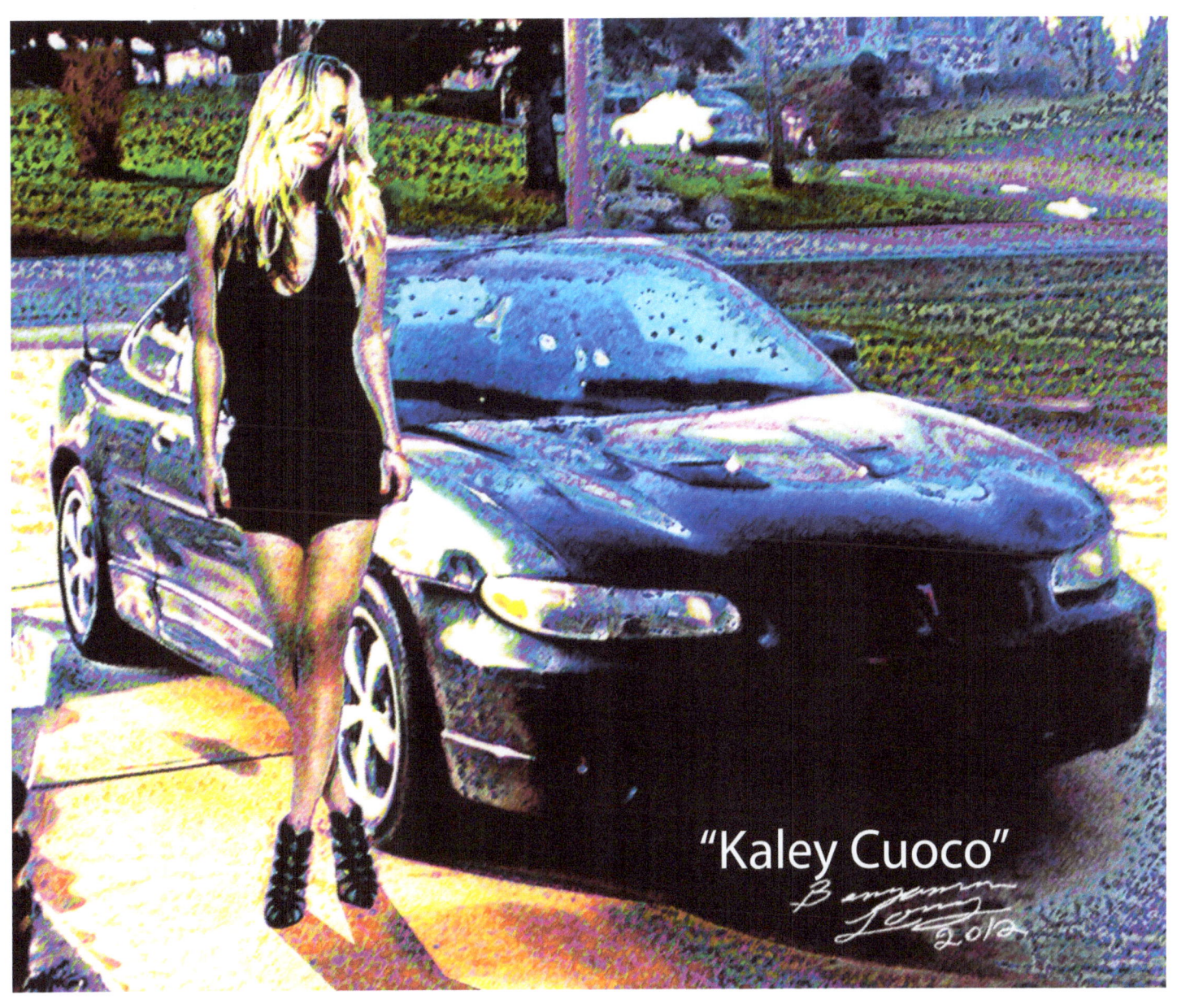

"Kaley Cuoco"

Model Rendering

Pelikan Ink/Colored Pencil

Illustration of a Model, One is done in a vivid Palette while the other is the natural drawing.

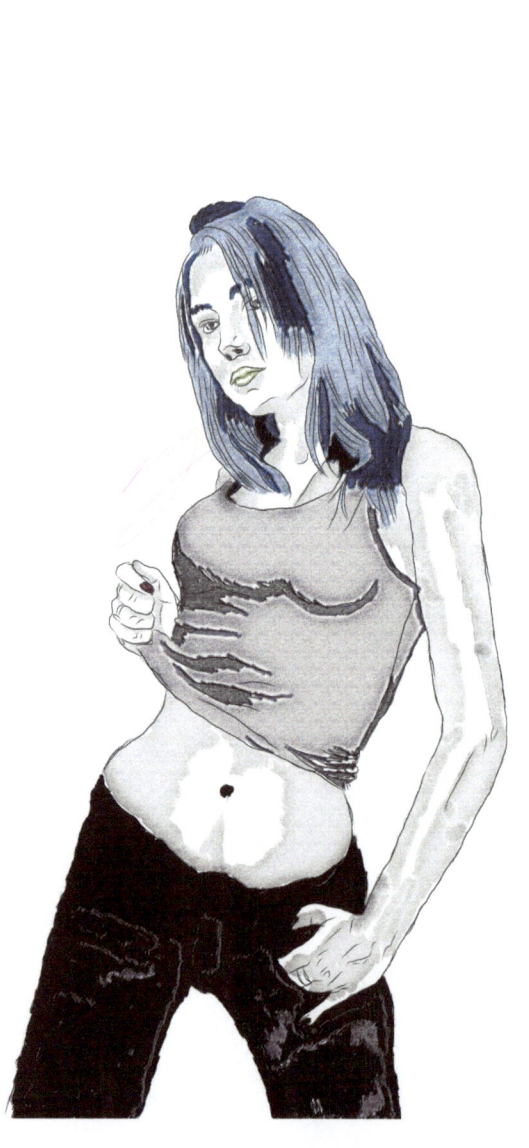

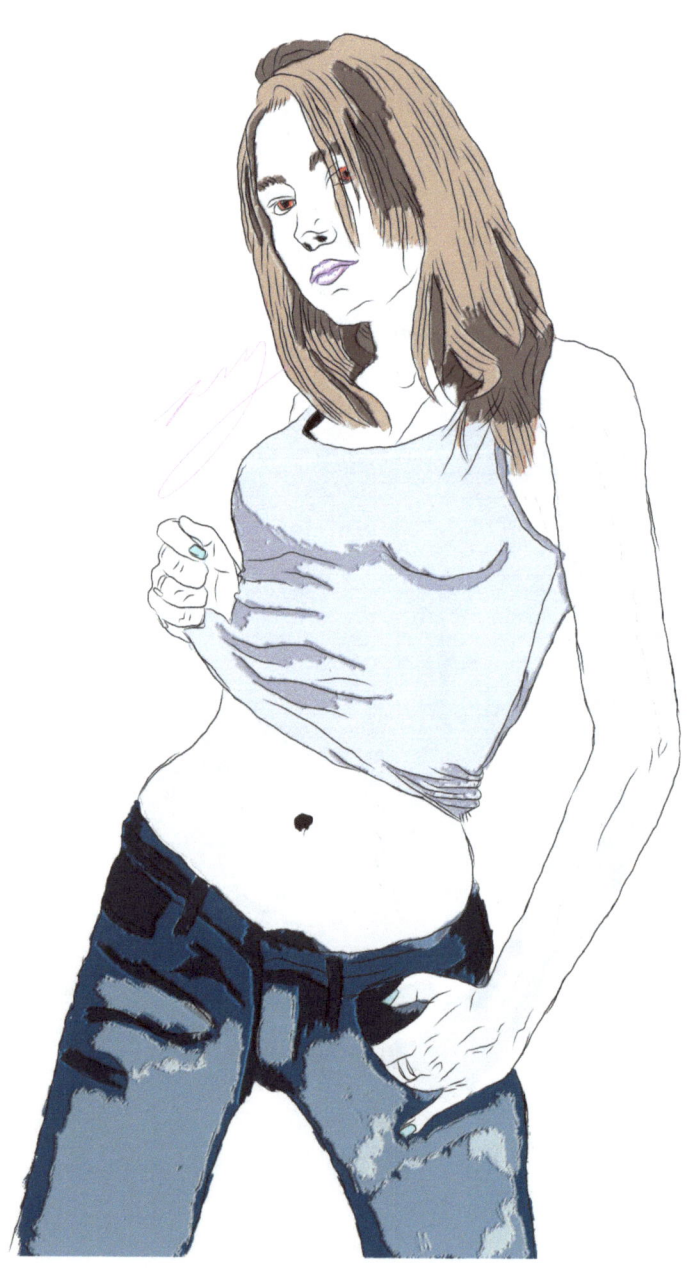

Pontiac Grand Prix

Pelikan Ink

Illustration of a Woman sitting on top of a 99 Grand Prix done in Pelikan Drawing ink.

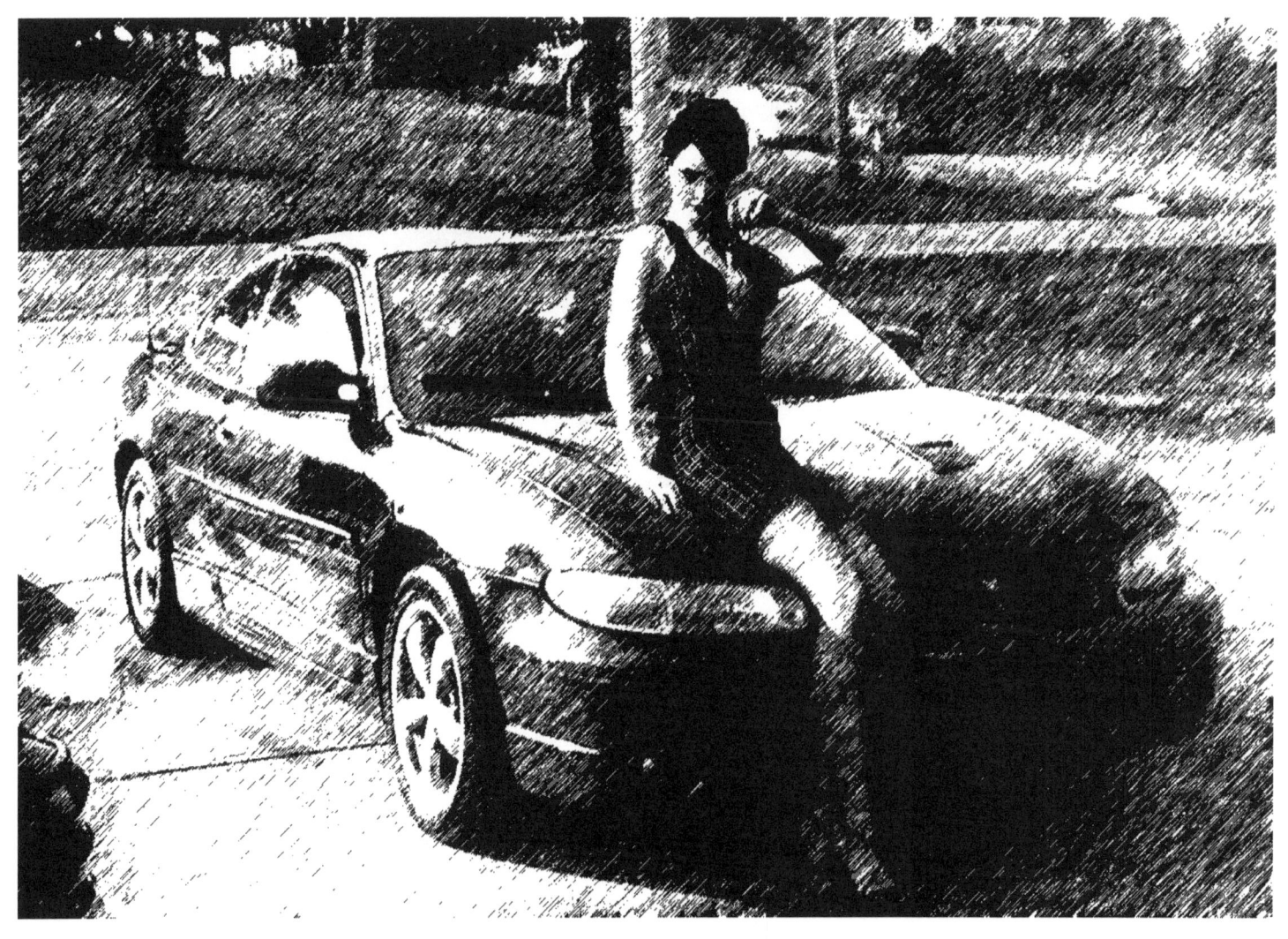

Woman on Log

Pelikan Ink/Colored Pencil

Illustration of a Woman on a Log.

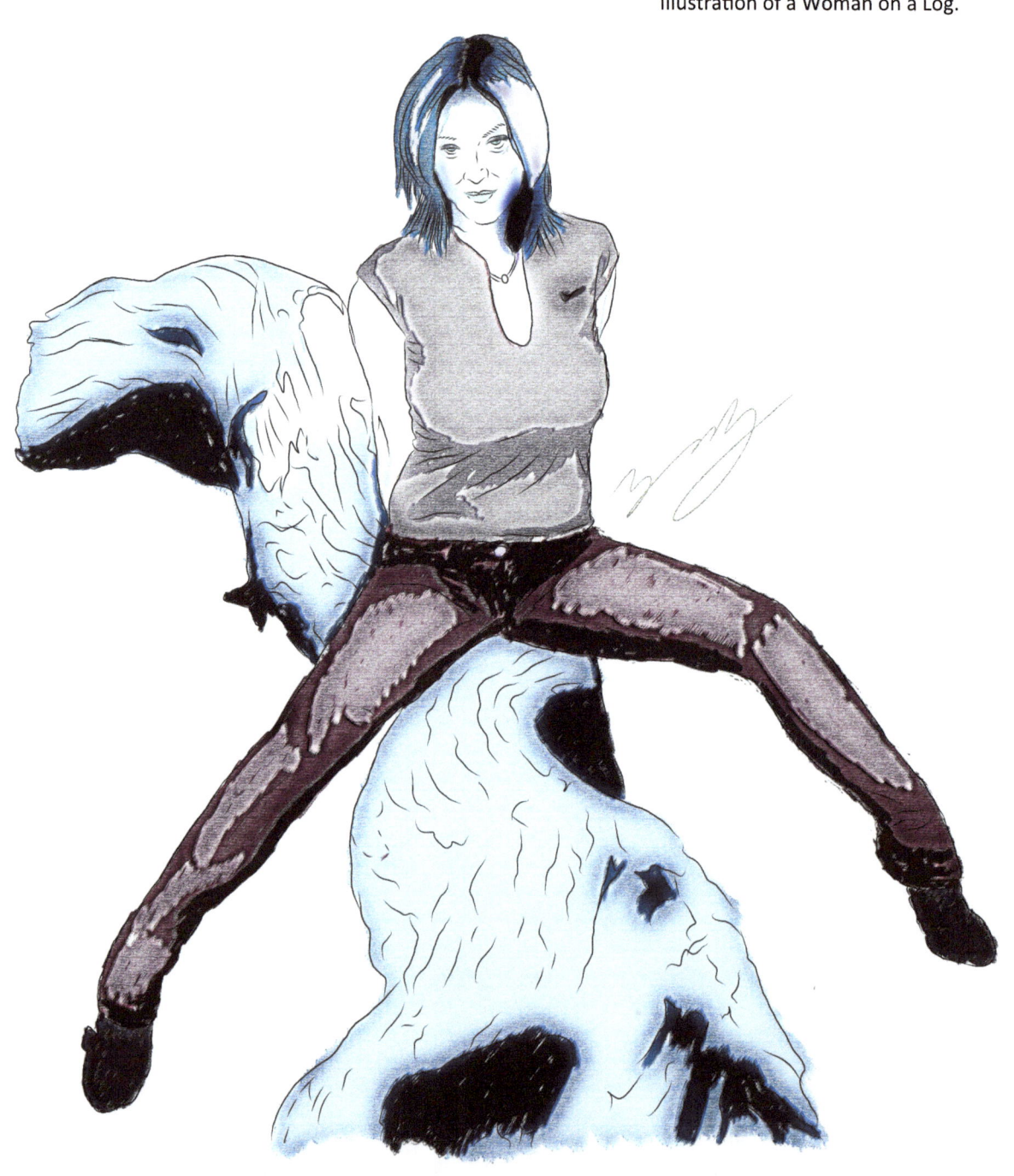

Lingerie

Pelikan Ink/Colored Pencil

Illustration of a Nude Woman dressed in lingerie.

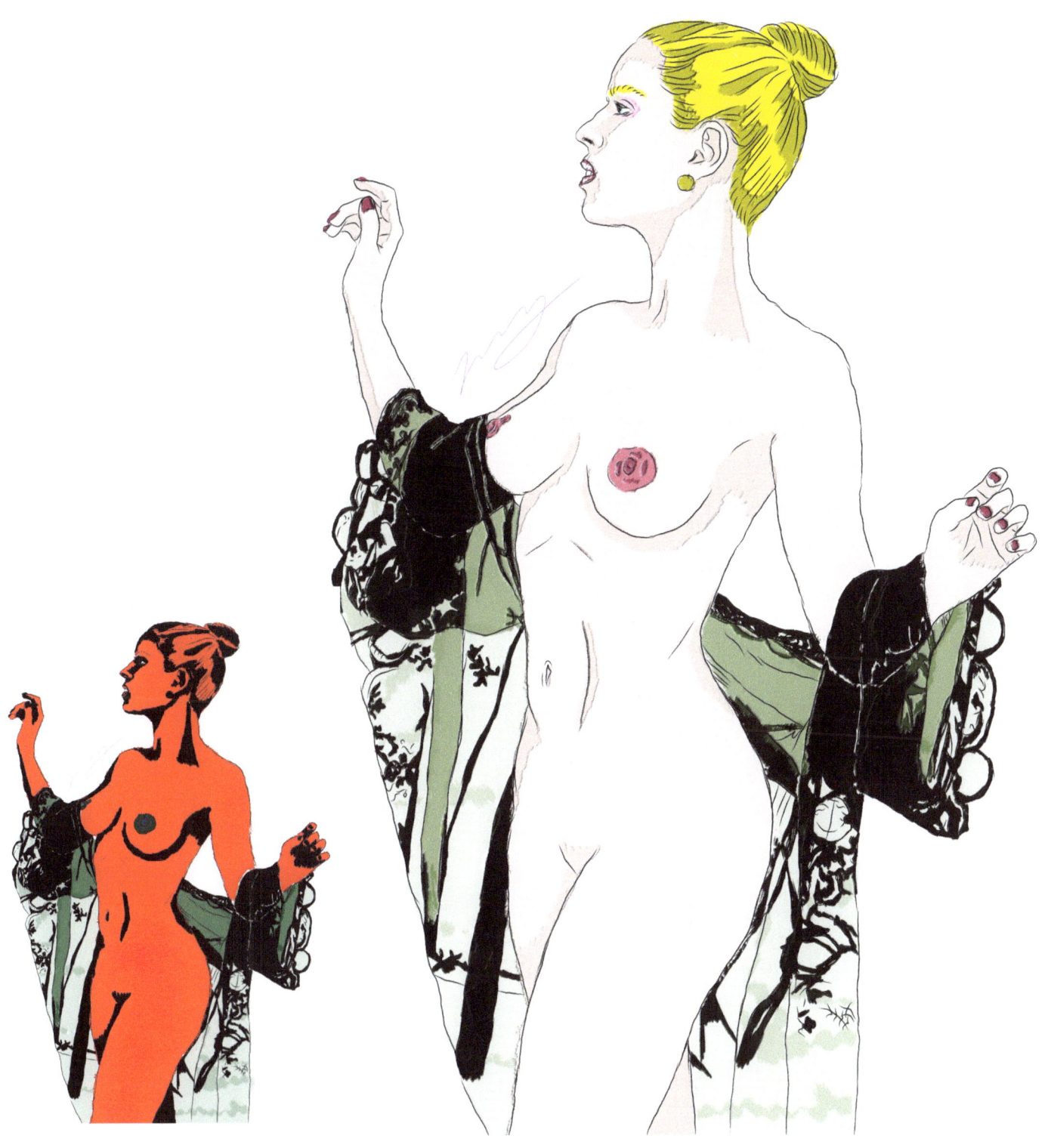

Mustang Fox Body

Pelikan Ink/Colored Pencil

Illustration of a Ford Mustang with a nude model on top of it.

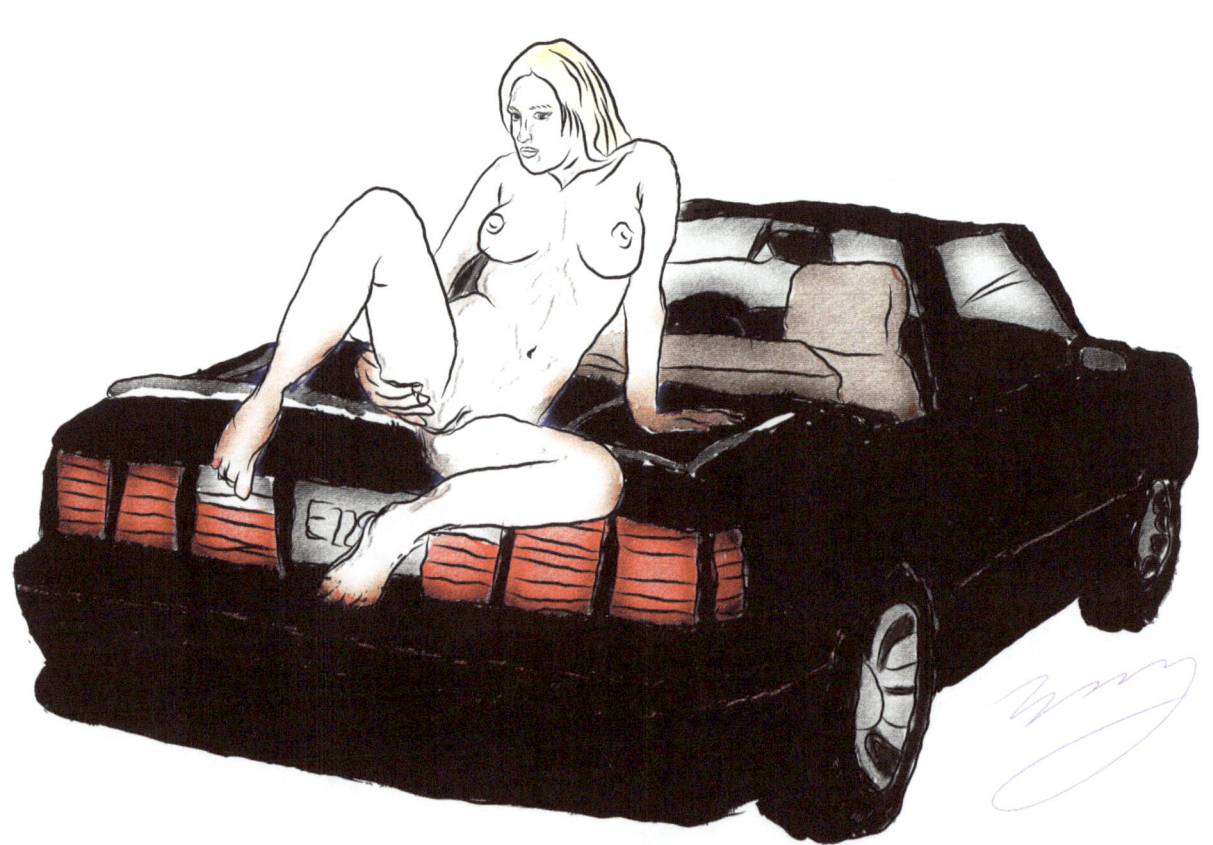

MUSTANG FOX BODY

ILLUSTRATED BY BENJAMIN LONG 2012

Nude Pose
Pelikan Ink/Colored Pencil

Illustration of a Nude Model lying on her back.

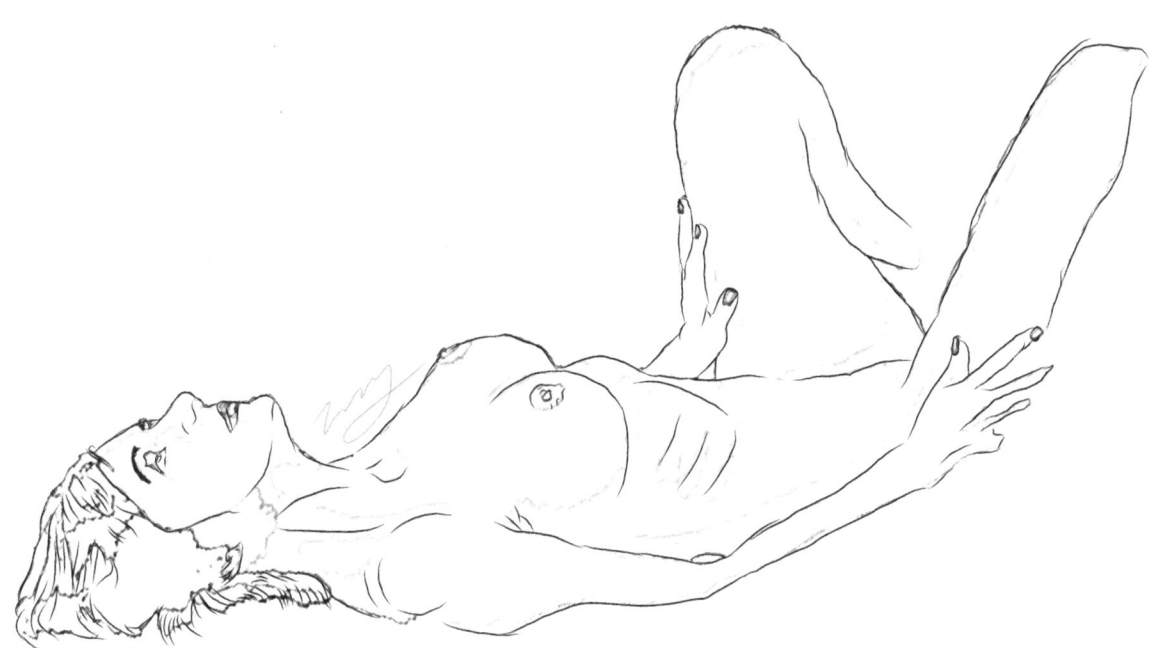

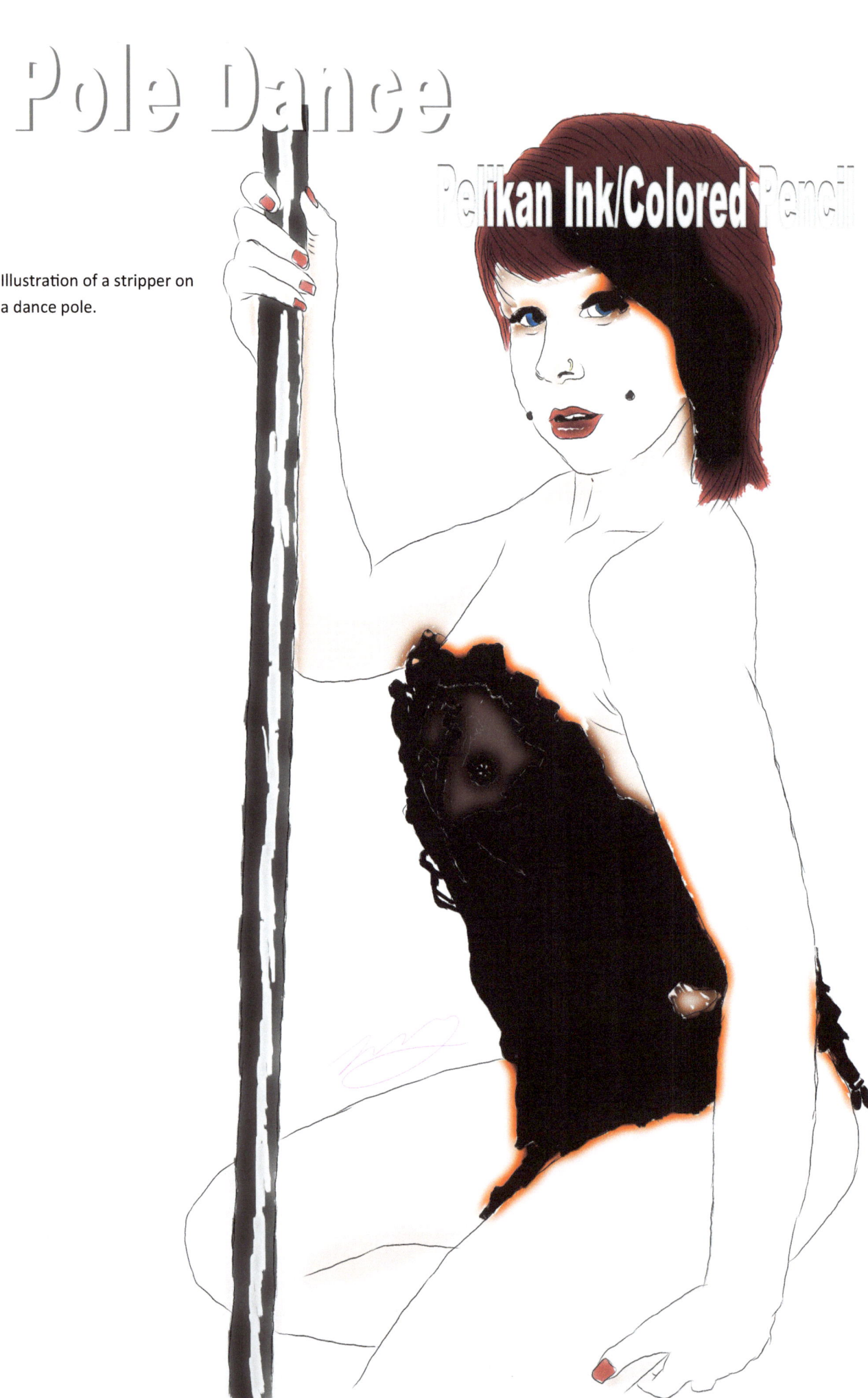

Pole Dance

Pelikan Ink/Colored Pencil

Illustration of a stripper on a dance pole.

Zombie Vision

Illustration of Actress Rose McGowan posing in front of vehicle with a zombie like effect added.

Digital Drawing/Painting

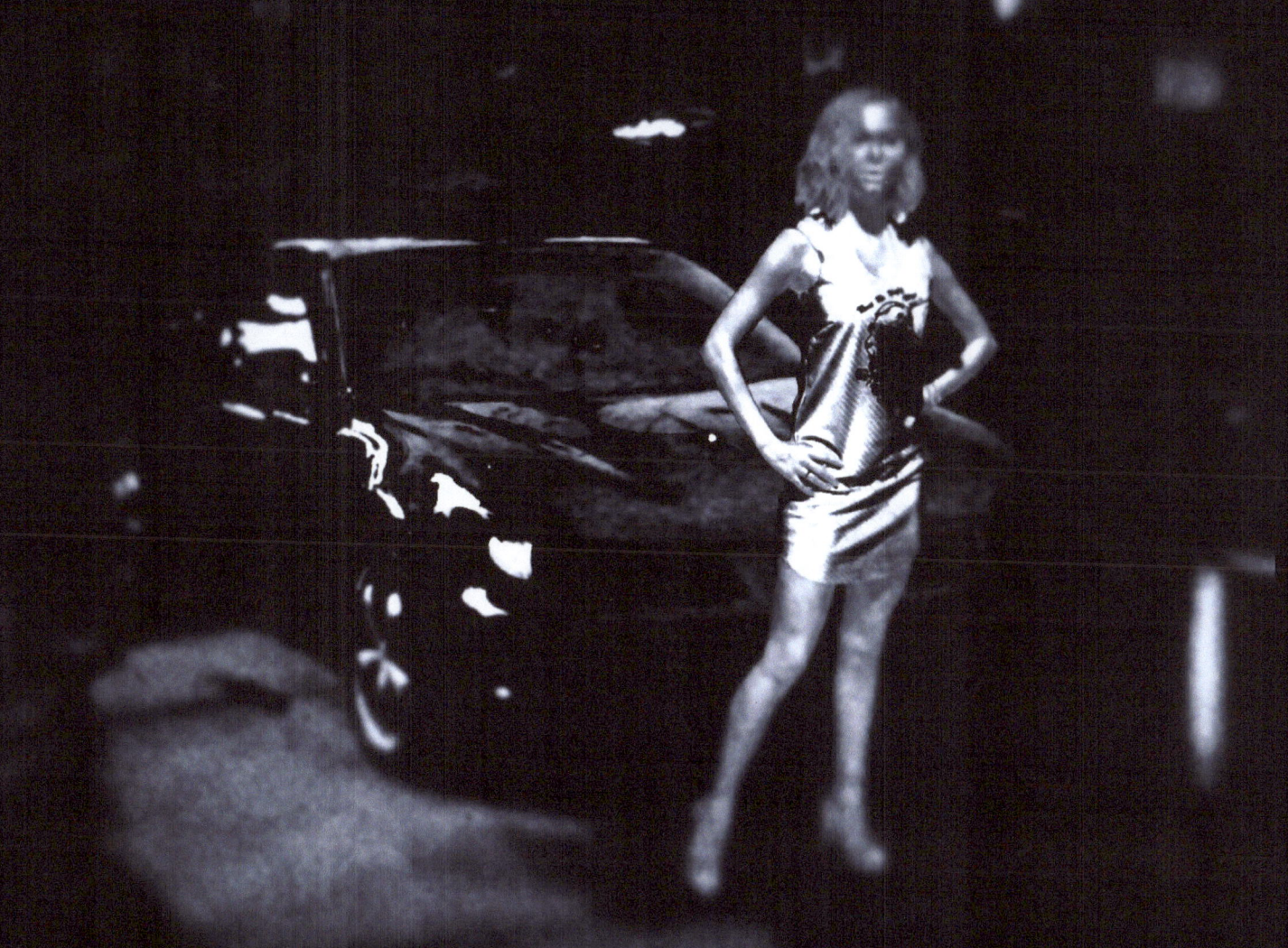

65 Mustang

Digital Drawing/ Painting

Illustration of Emma Starr posing in front of a 65 Ford Mustang Convertible.

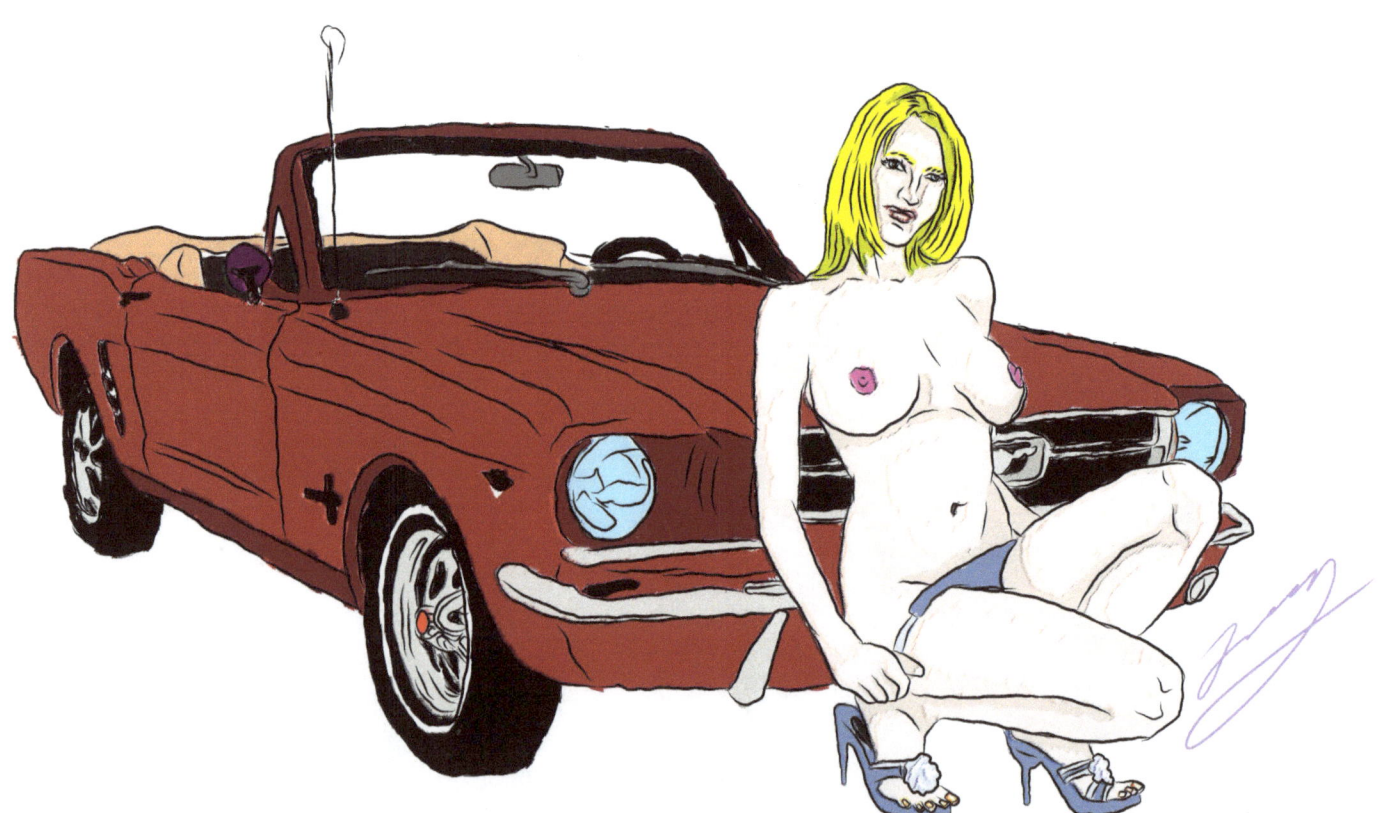

Valentine's Card

Digital Drawing/Painting

Illustration of a Valentine's Card that I did for the Holidays.

Happy Valentine's Day

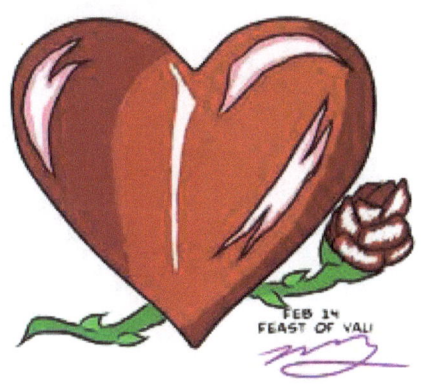

For all the love you give

This heart is for you...

Illustration by Benjamin Long © 2012

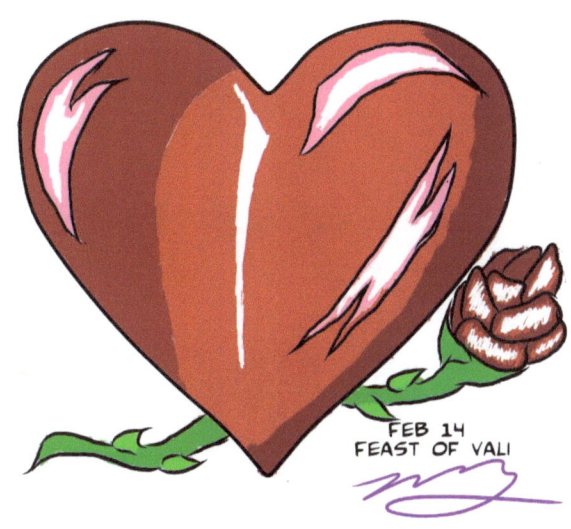

Vin Diesel

Illustration of in Diesel done in a Monochrome style.

Digital Drawing/Painting

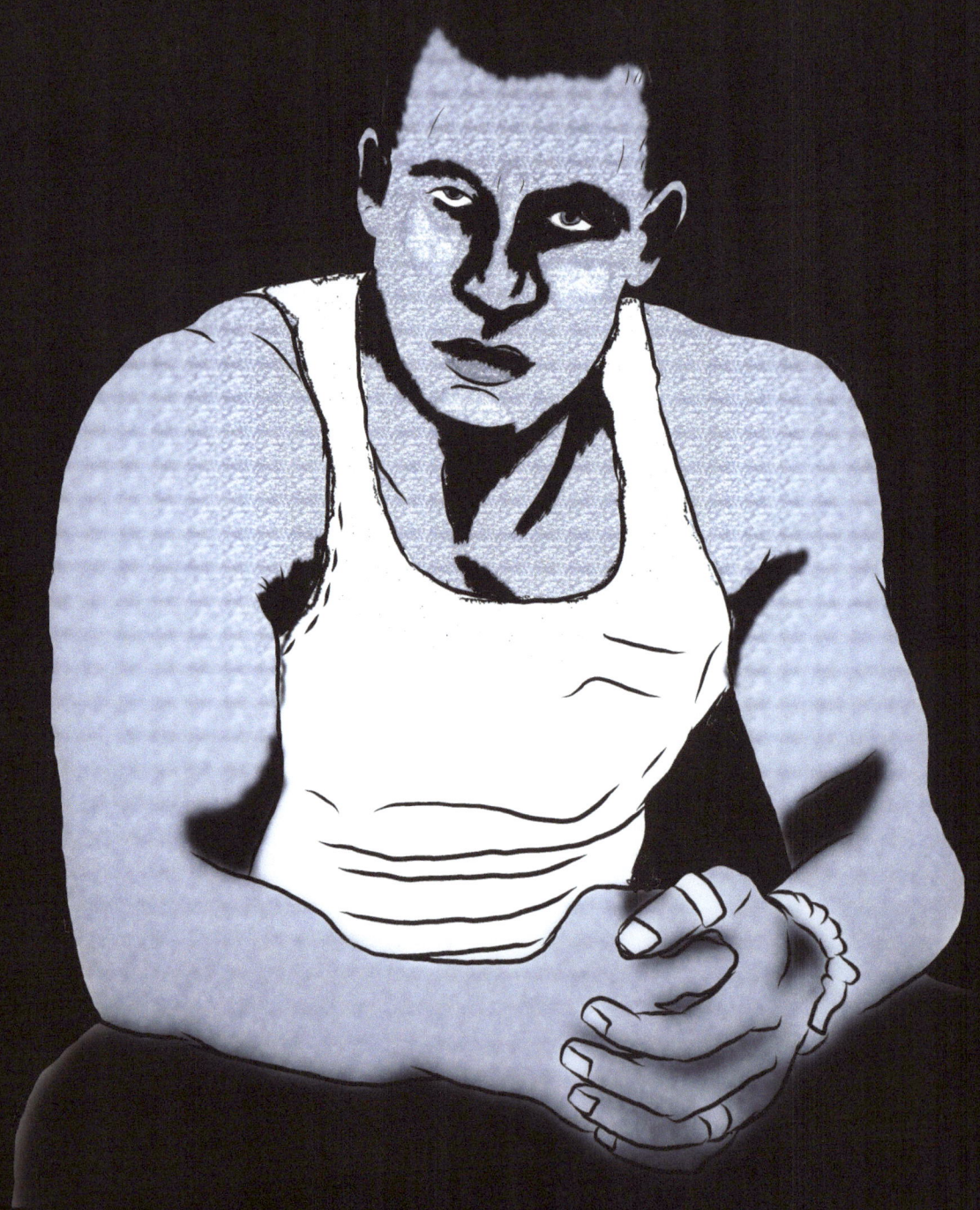

Wet Shirt

Illustration of a woman in a wet shirt.

Pelikan Ink

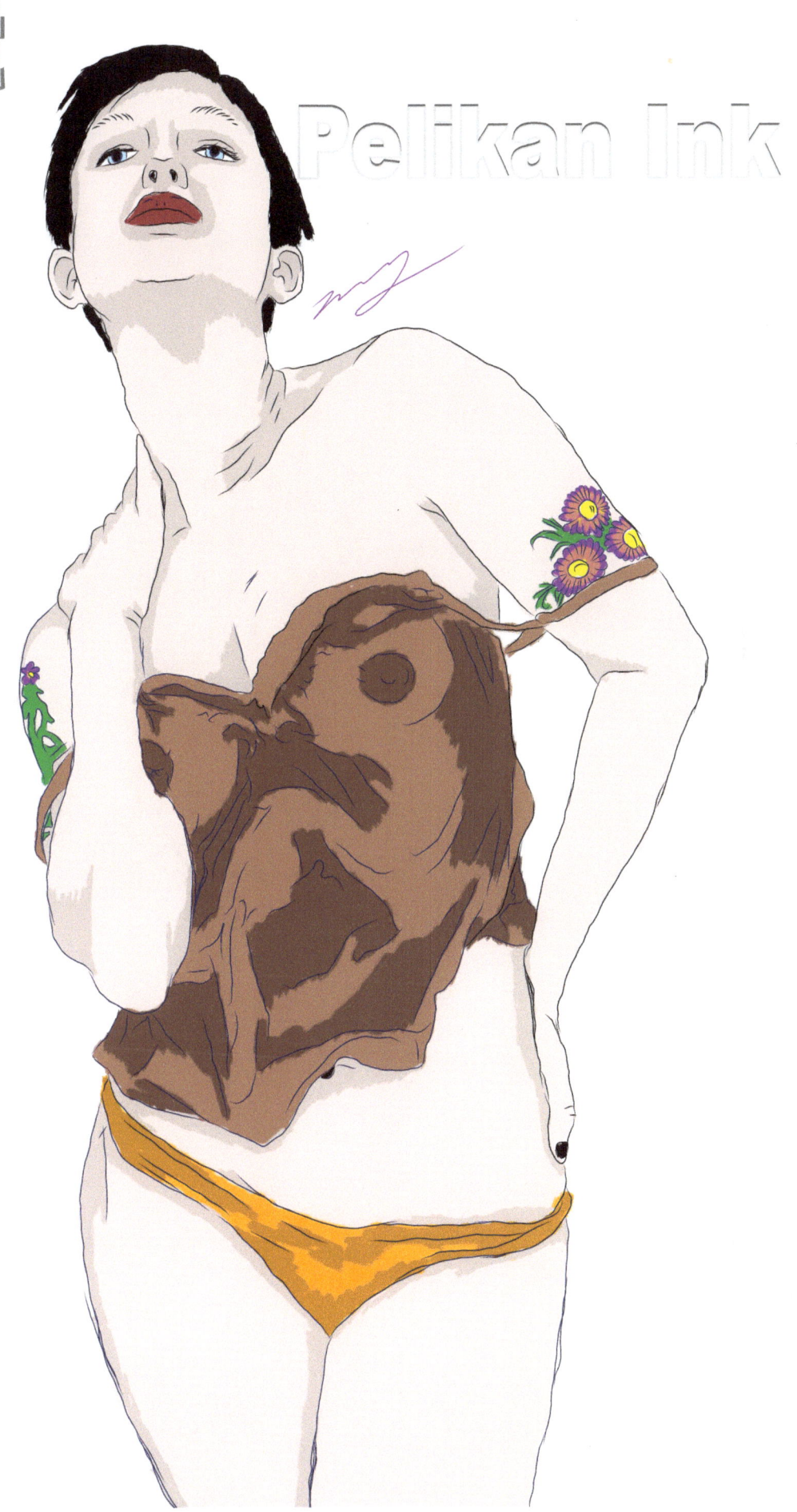

Woman and Dog

Digital Drawing/Painting

Illustration of a Dog tugging
at a woman's underwear

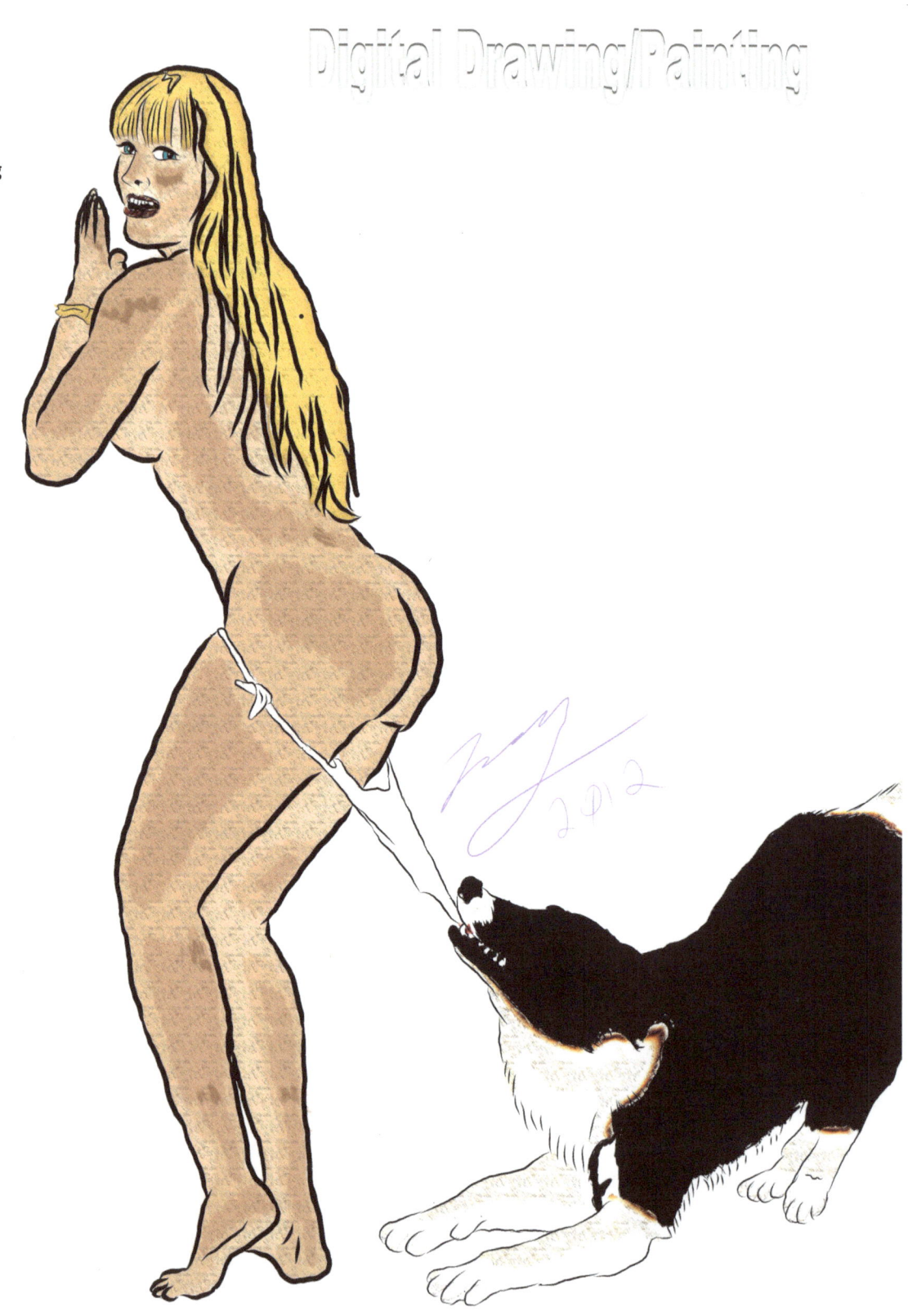

Woman on Couch

Illustration of a Woman on couch, done with Pelikan and digital rendering methods.

Digital Drawing/Painting

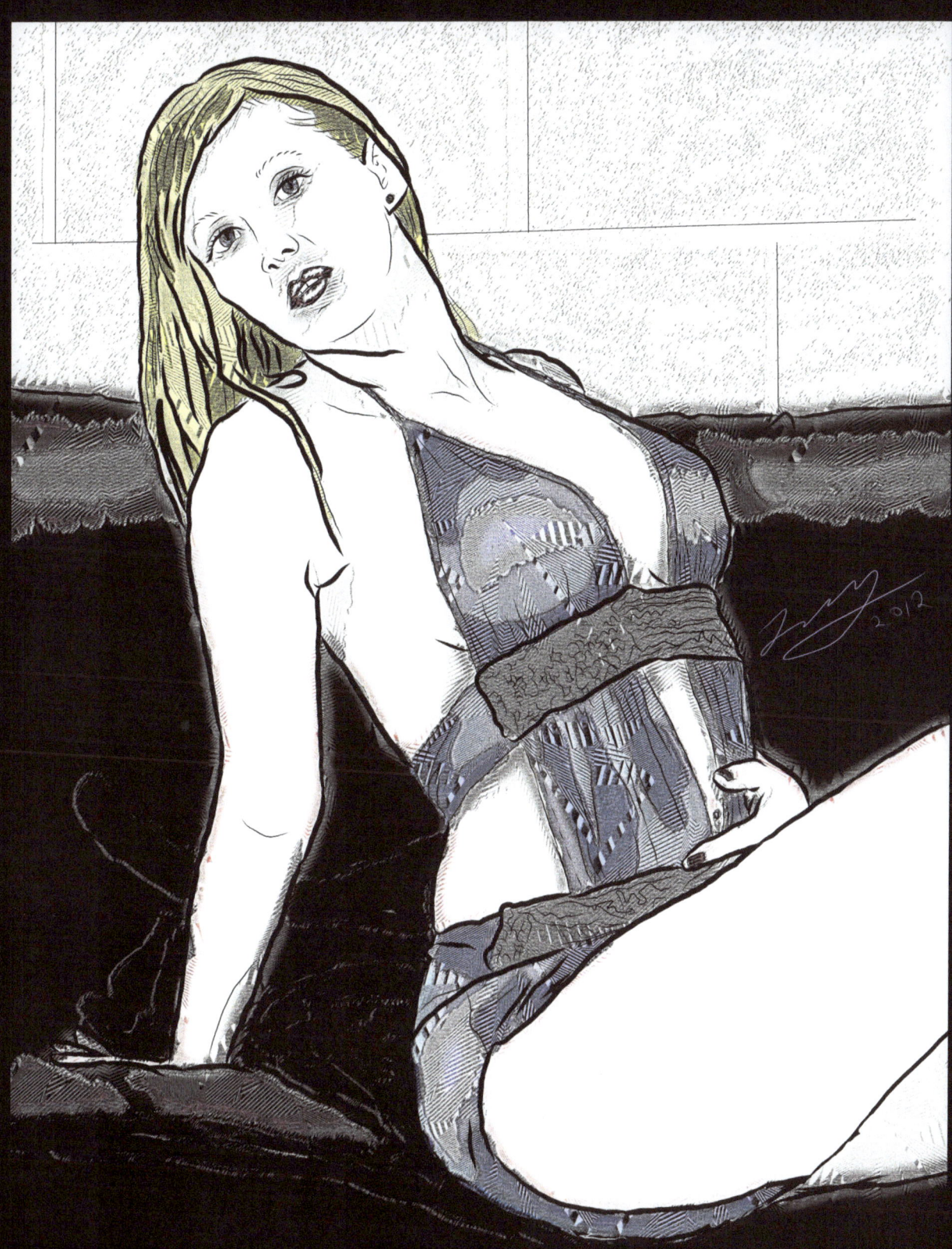

Ferret

Digital Line Art/ Digital coloring

Illustration of a Ferret that was done as
a commission for a customer.

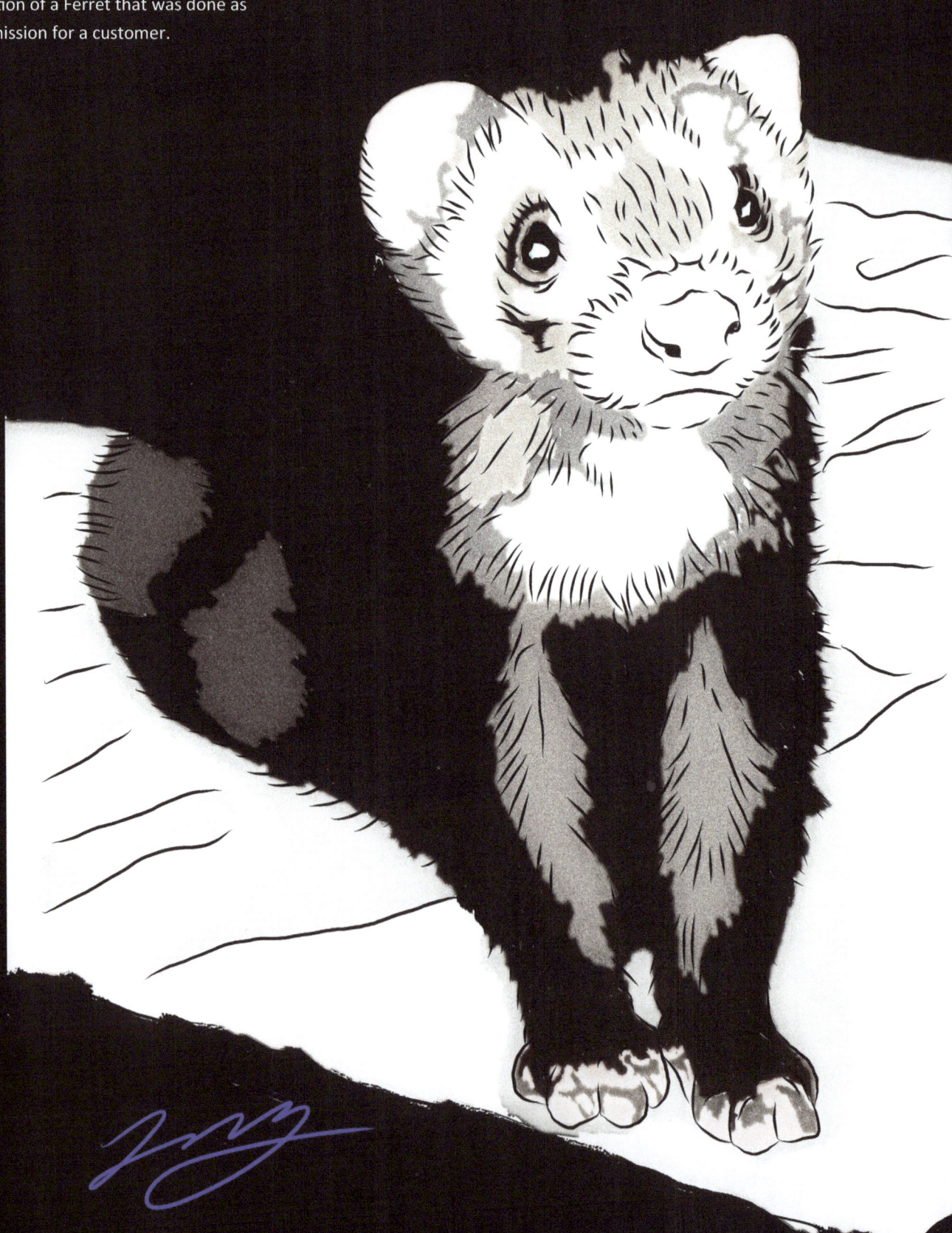

Grand Prix Sketch #1
Mechanical Pencil

Sketch Work for my Rose McGowan Illustration

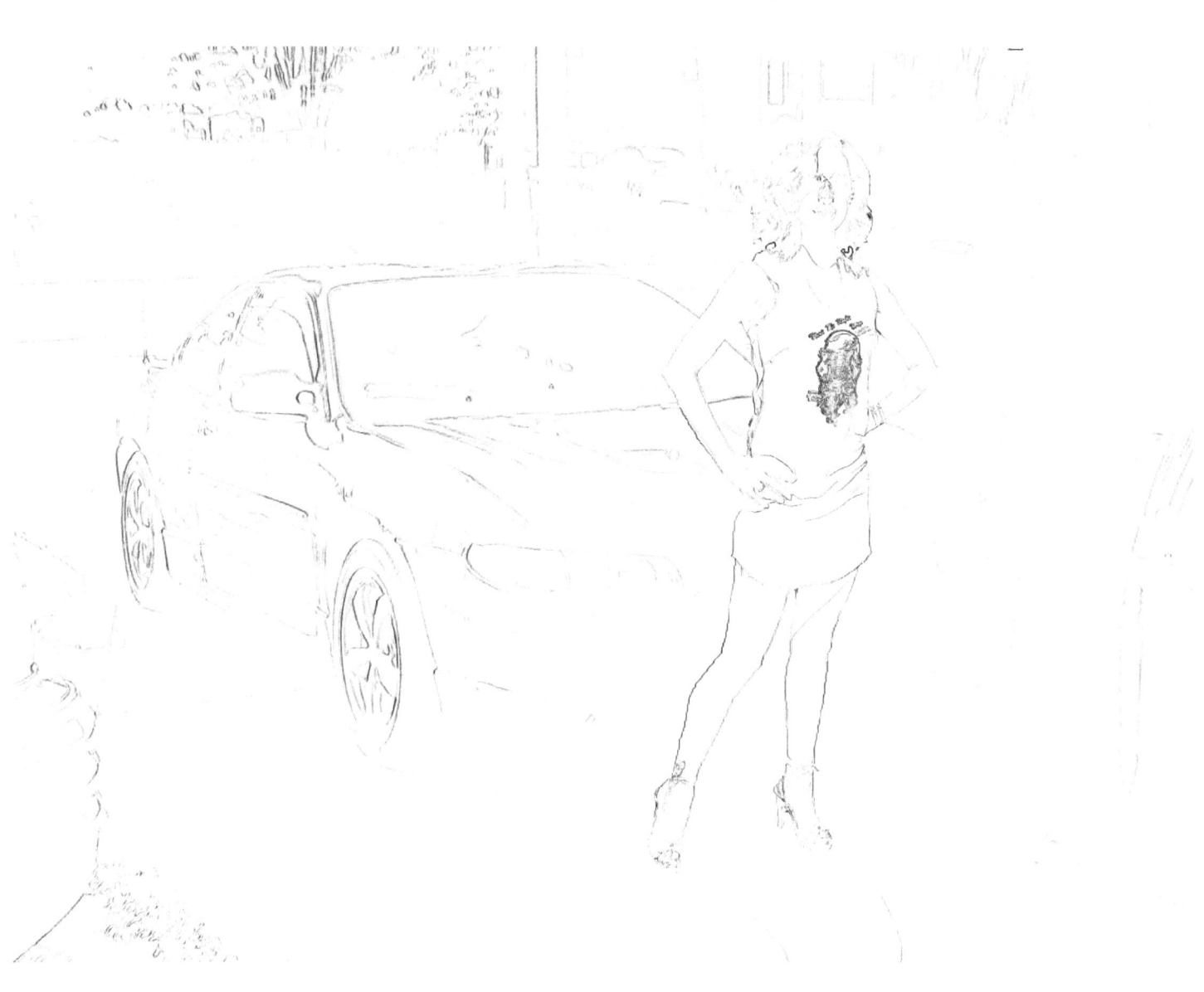

Grand Prix Shine

Pelikan Ink/Digital Color

Illustration of Rose McGowan posing in front of a 99 Grand Prix. Rendered with a golden shine effect over it to give it a more bronze feel.

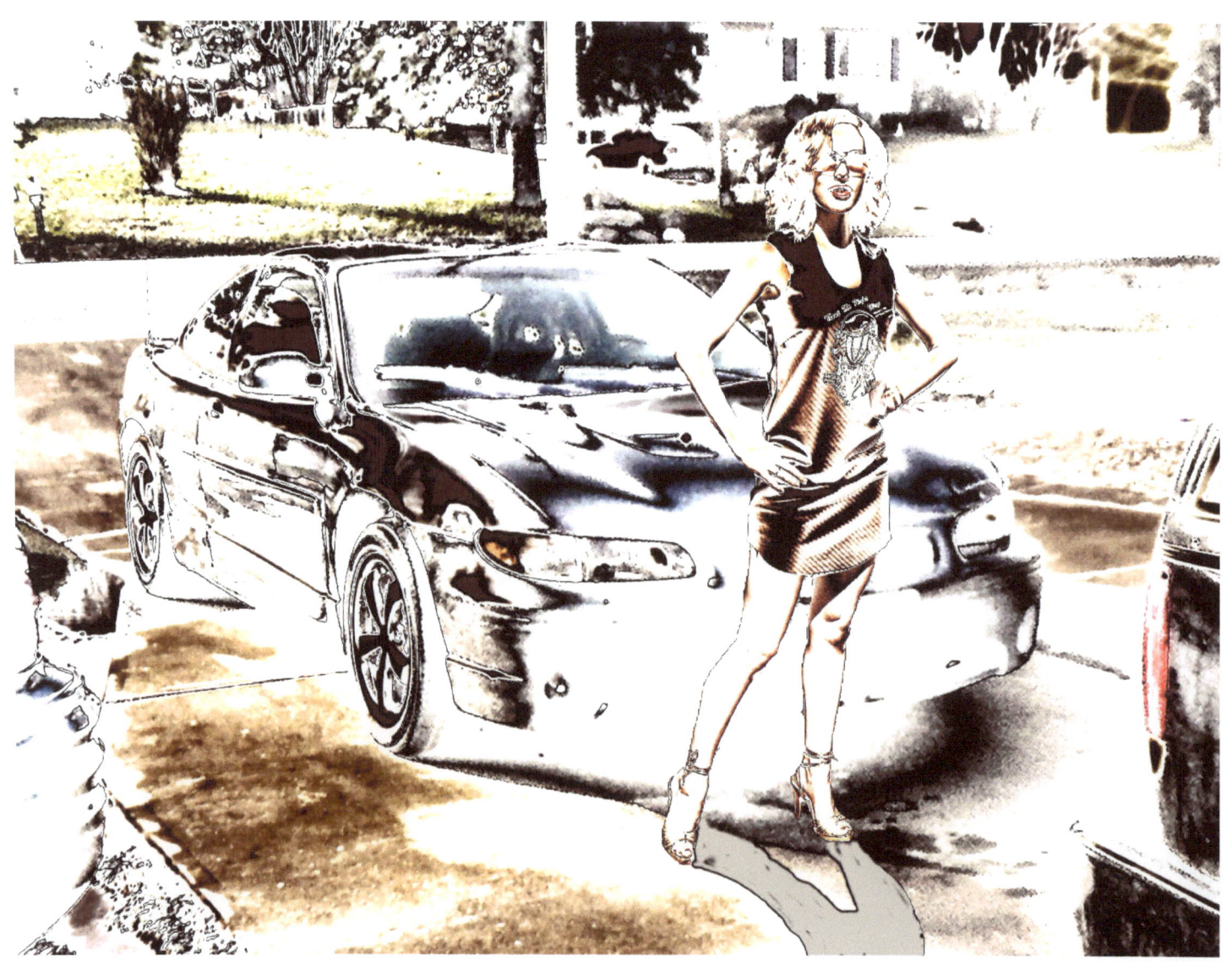

Cuoco Sketch
Mechanical Pencil

Preliminary Sketch of Kaley Cuoco posing in front of a Pontiac grand prix.

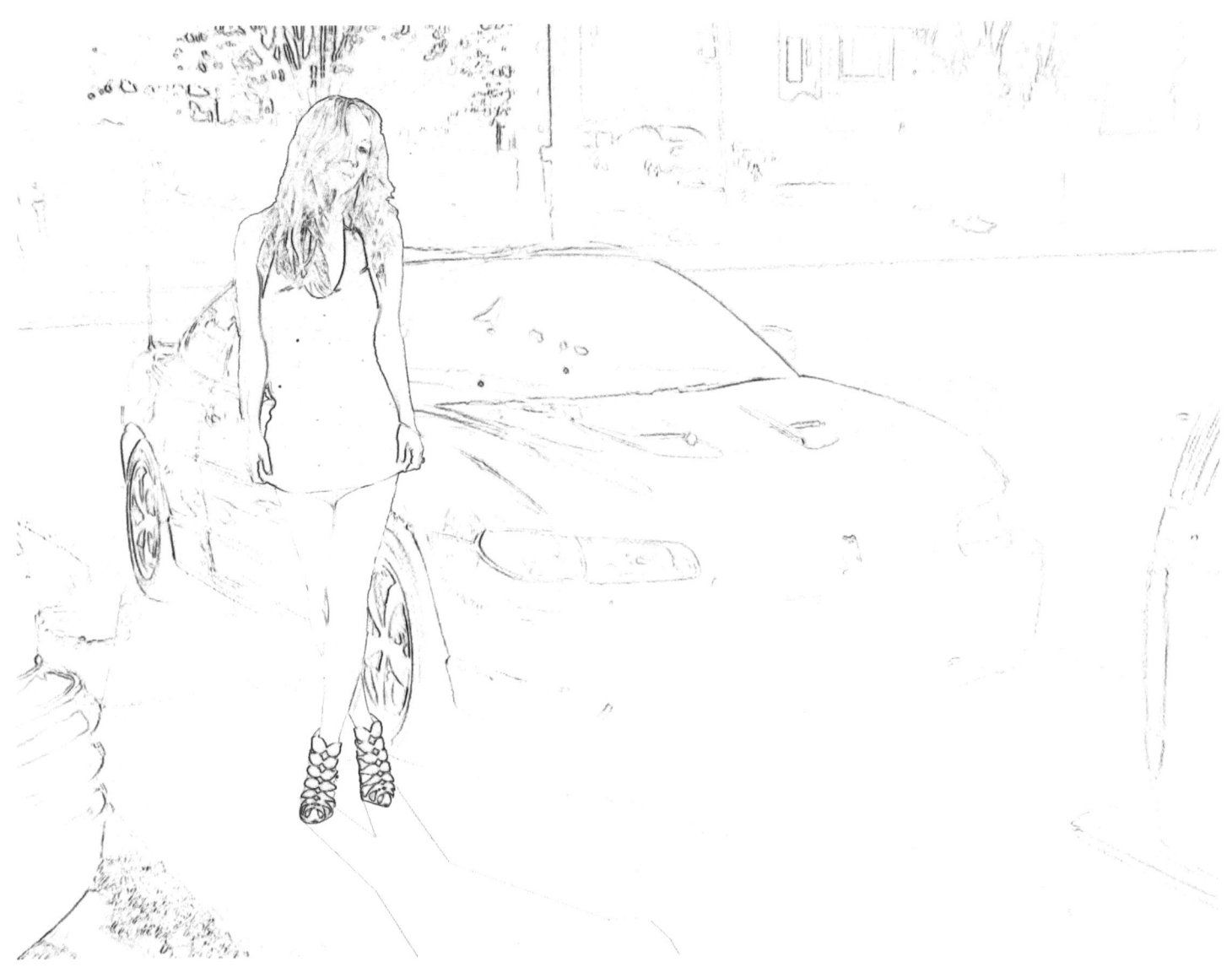

Frozen Model

Pelikan Ink/Digital Color

Illustration of Kaley Cuoco with a frozen effect added to give it an iced over feel.

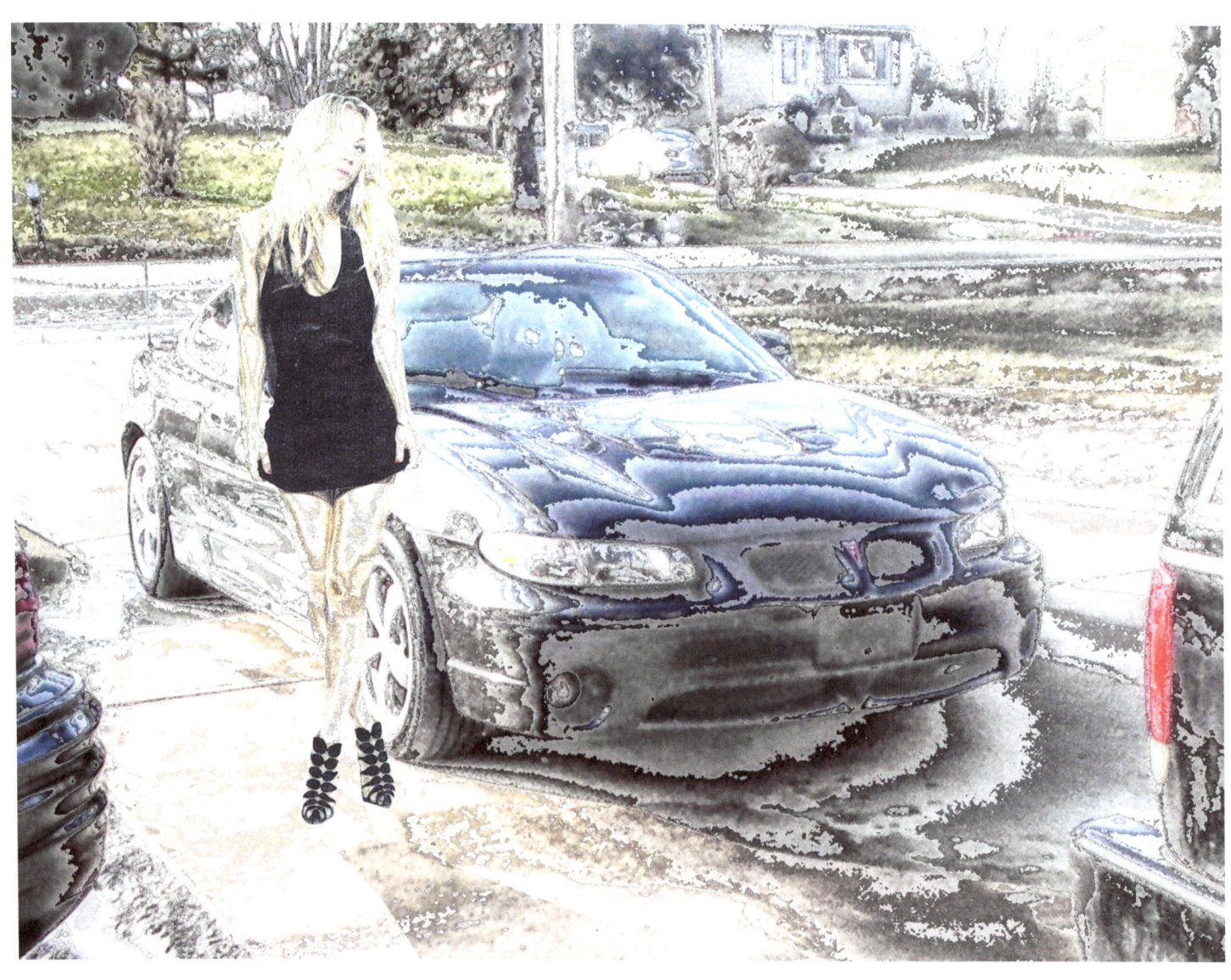

Rose Solar Flare
Photo Manipulation

I created this model design in Photoshop so that I could use it as a base model pic for the other works I created off this design.

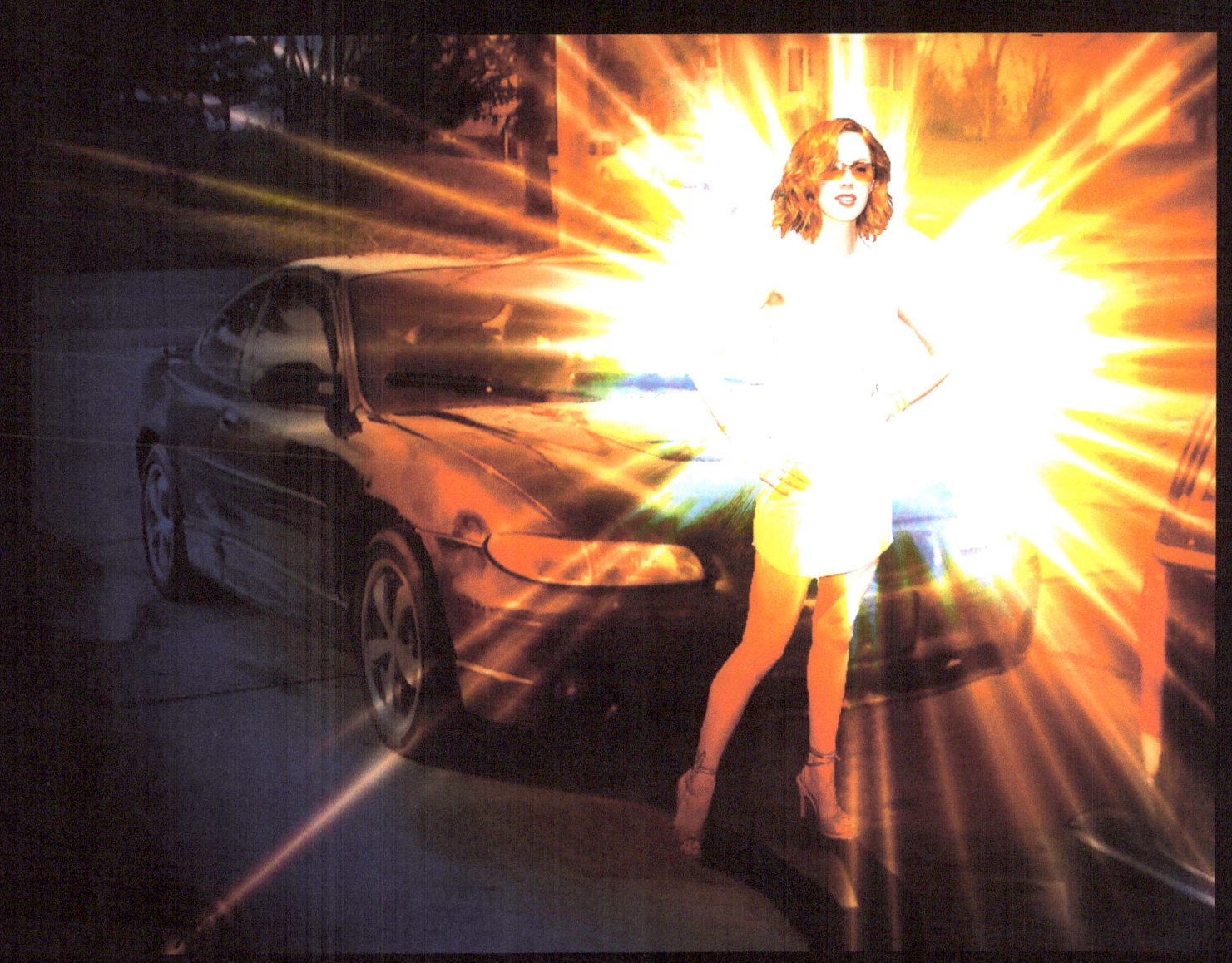

Mustang Contrast

Illustration of a 65 Mustang with a slight contrast adjustment

Pelikan Ink/Digital Color

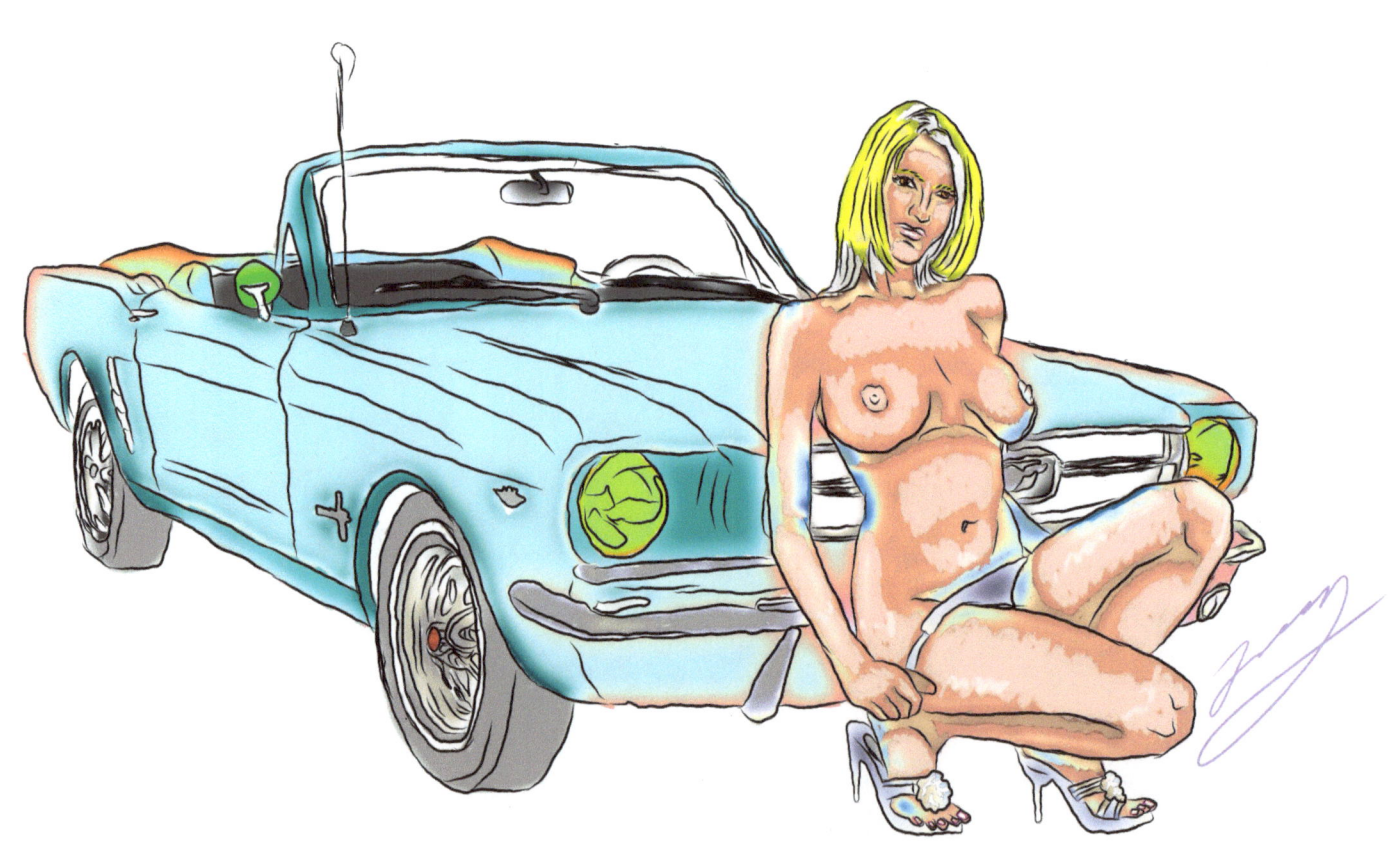

Wet Shirt Contrast

Pelikan Ink/ Digital Color

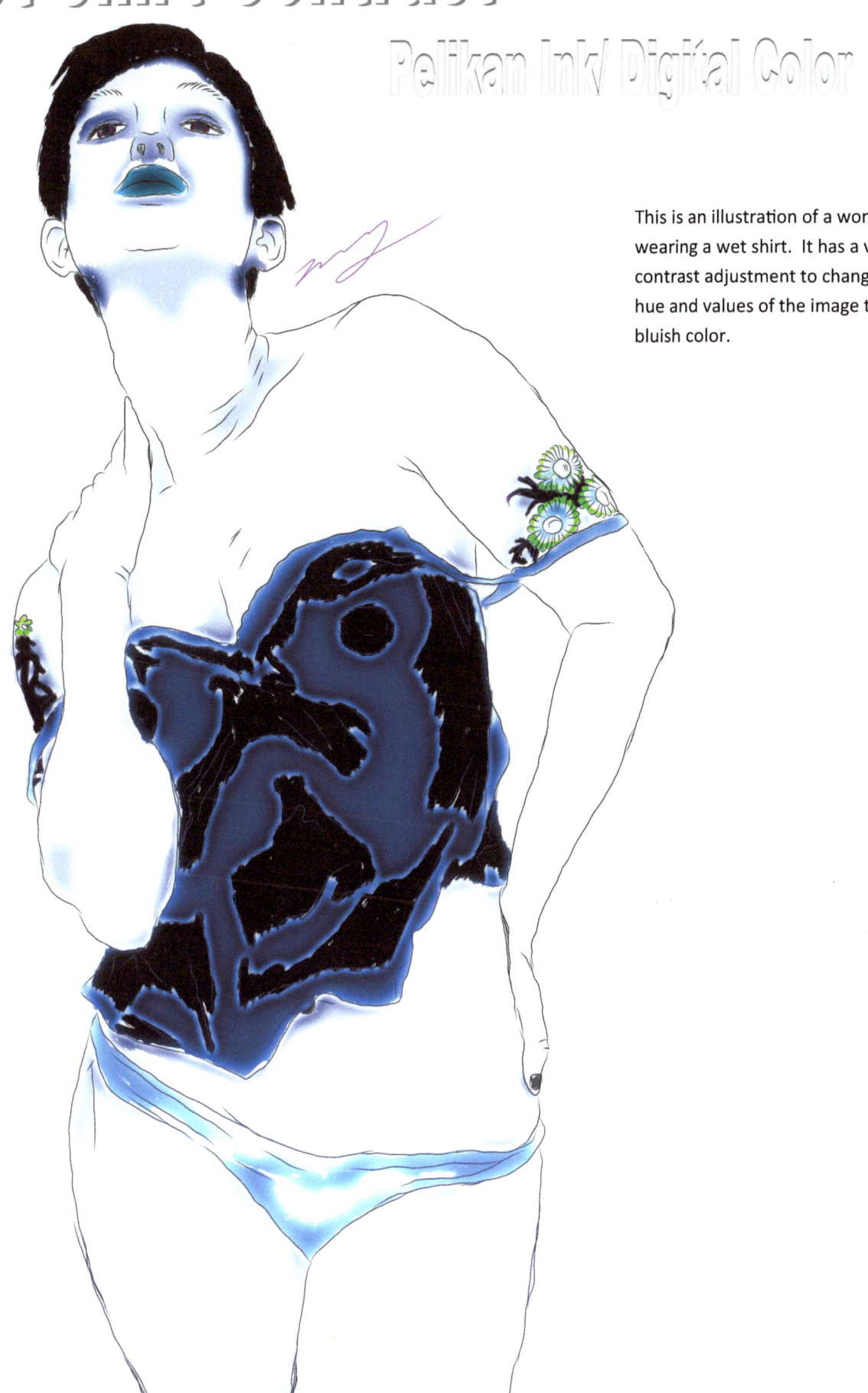

This is an illustration of a woman wearing a wet shirt. It has a vivid contrast adjustment to change the hue and values of the image to a bluish color.

Nude Pose
Digital Drawing

Illustration of a Nude Model on her back. The top is a luminance drawing and the bottom is a Gold Shine drawing.

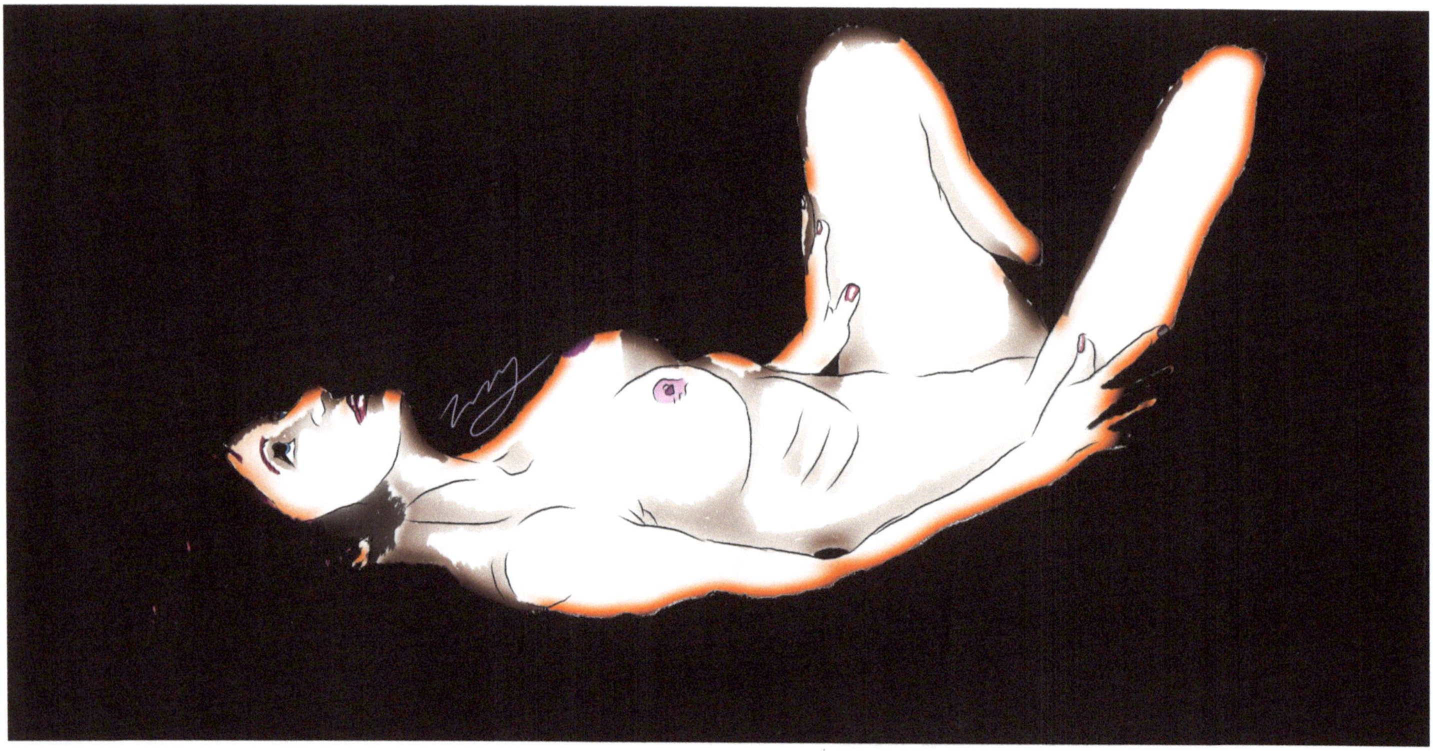

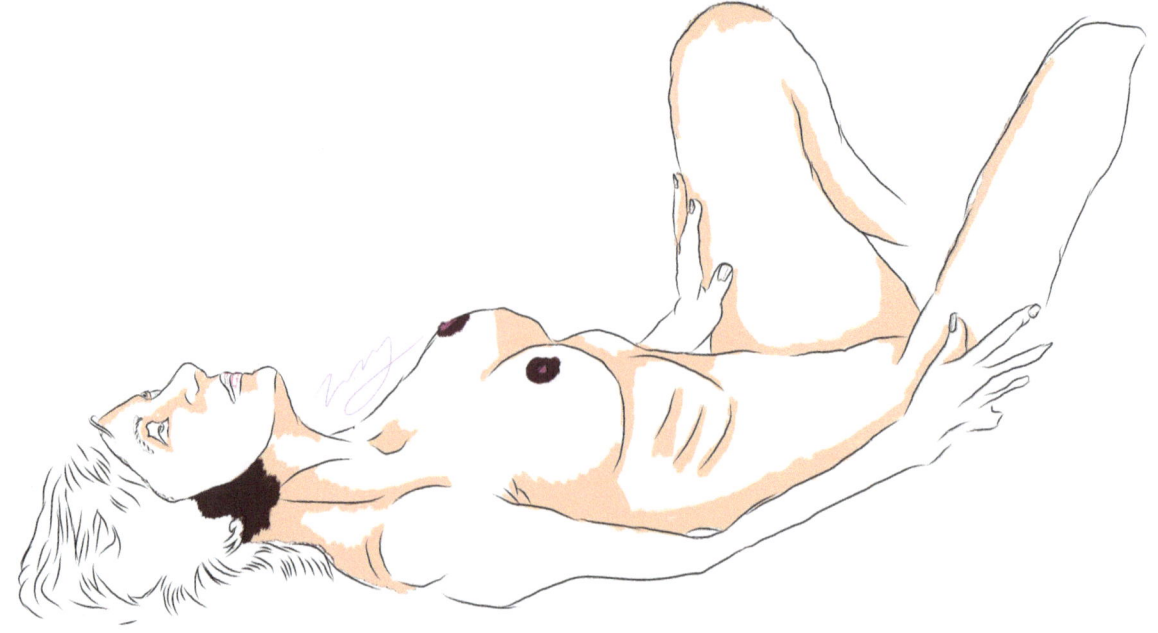

Girl on Log Natural

Illustration of a girl on a log using a realistic color palette.

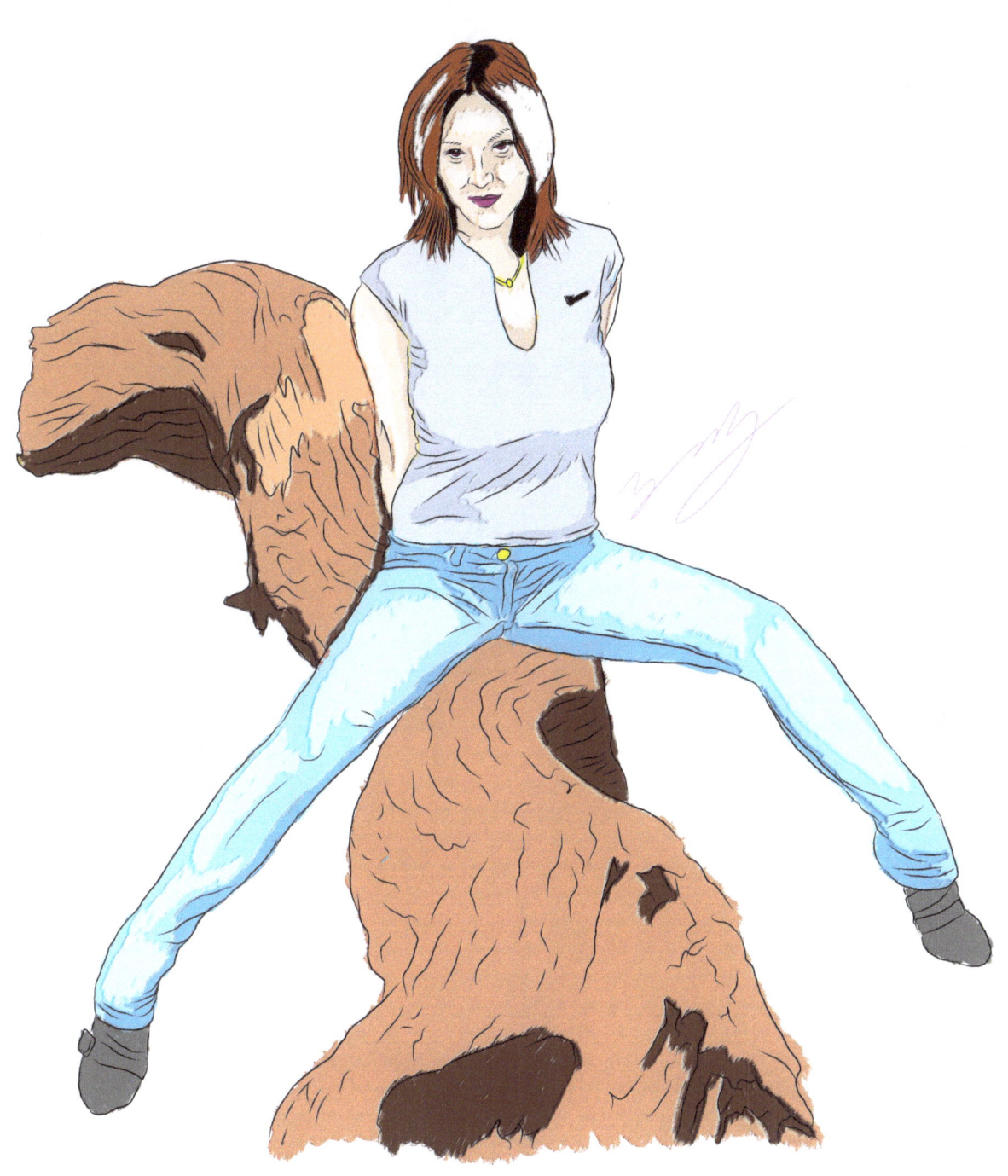

Blood Frenzy

Digital Drawing

This is a manipulation of a drawing that I did last month

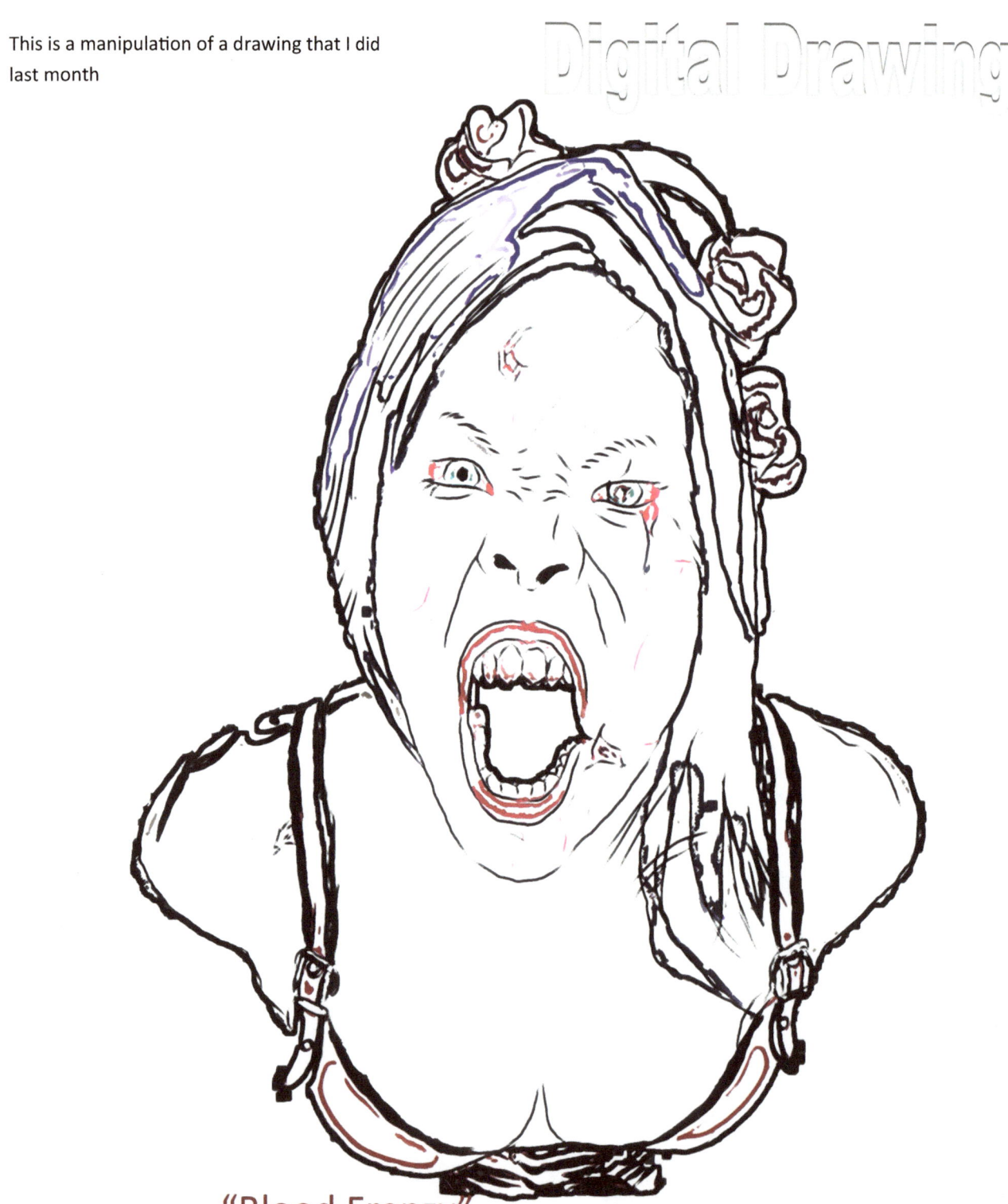

"Blood Frenzy"
Benjamin Long
Copyright 2012 All rights reserved
http:/whitewolfheathen.deviantart.com

Indian Family
Digital Drawing

This is an illustration of a family photo that I was hired to do.

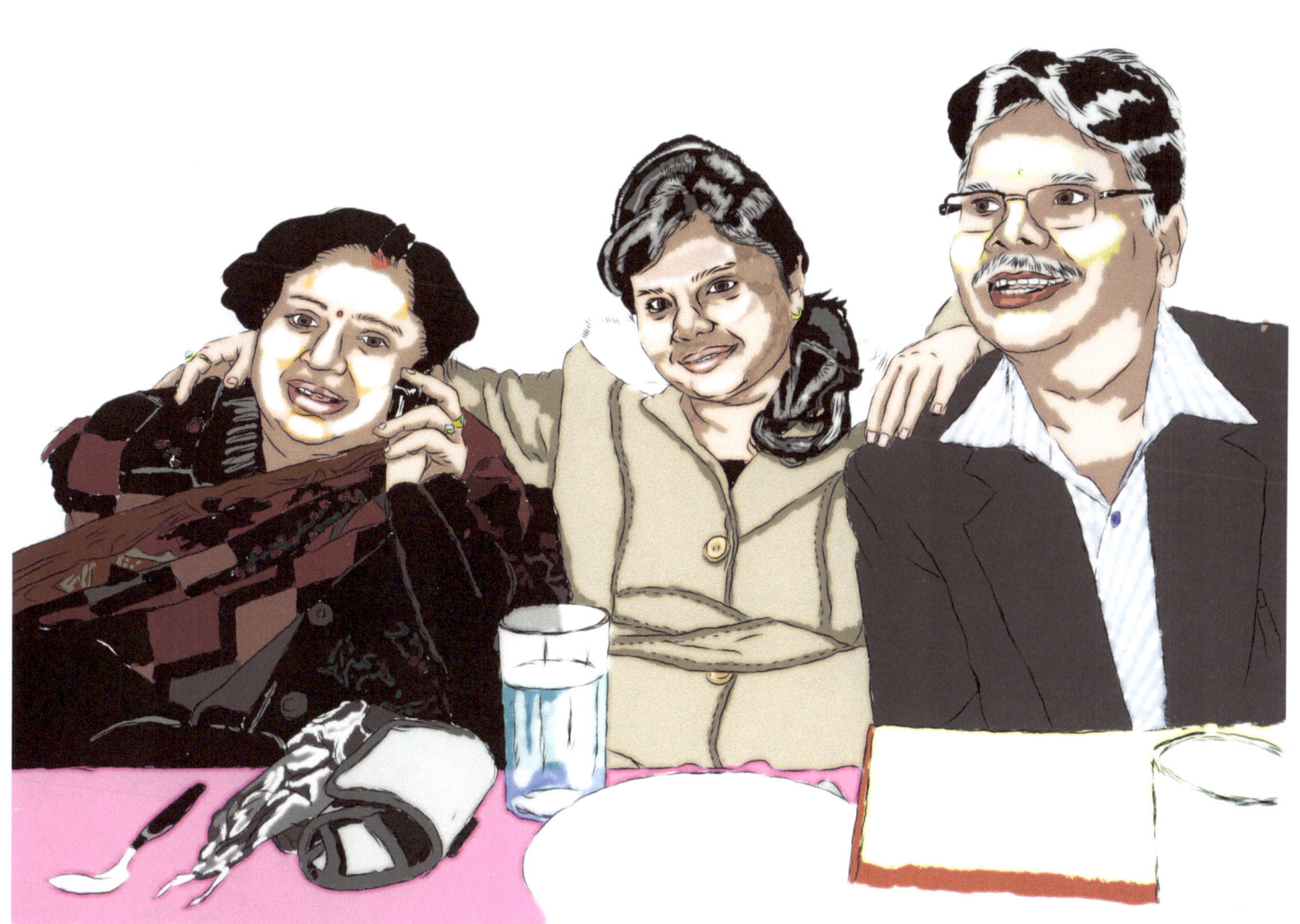

Girl Eating

Illustration of a Woman eating a bowl of soup, done as a commission.

Digital Drawing

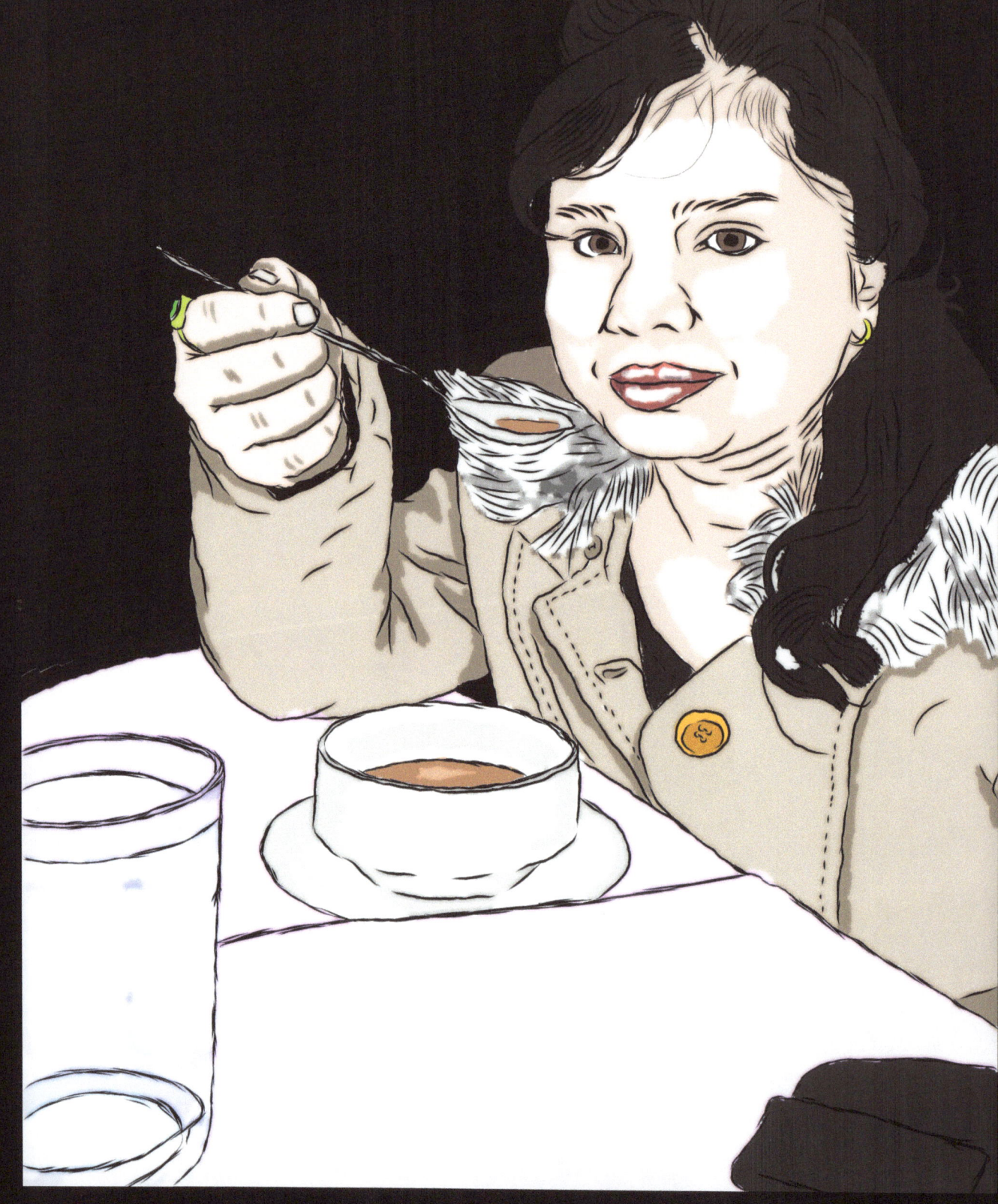

Woman and Cat   Digital Drawing

Illustration of a Woman Holding a Cat

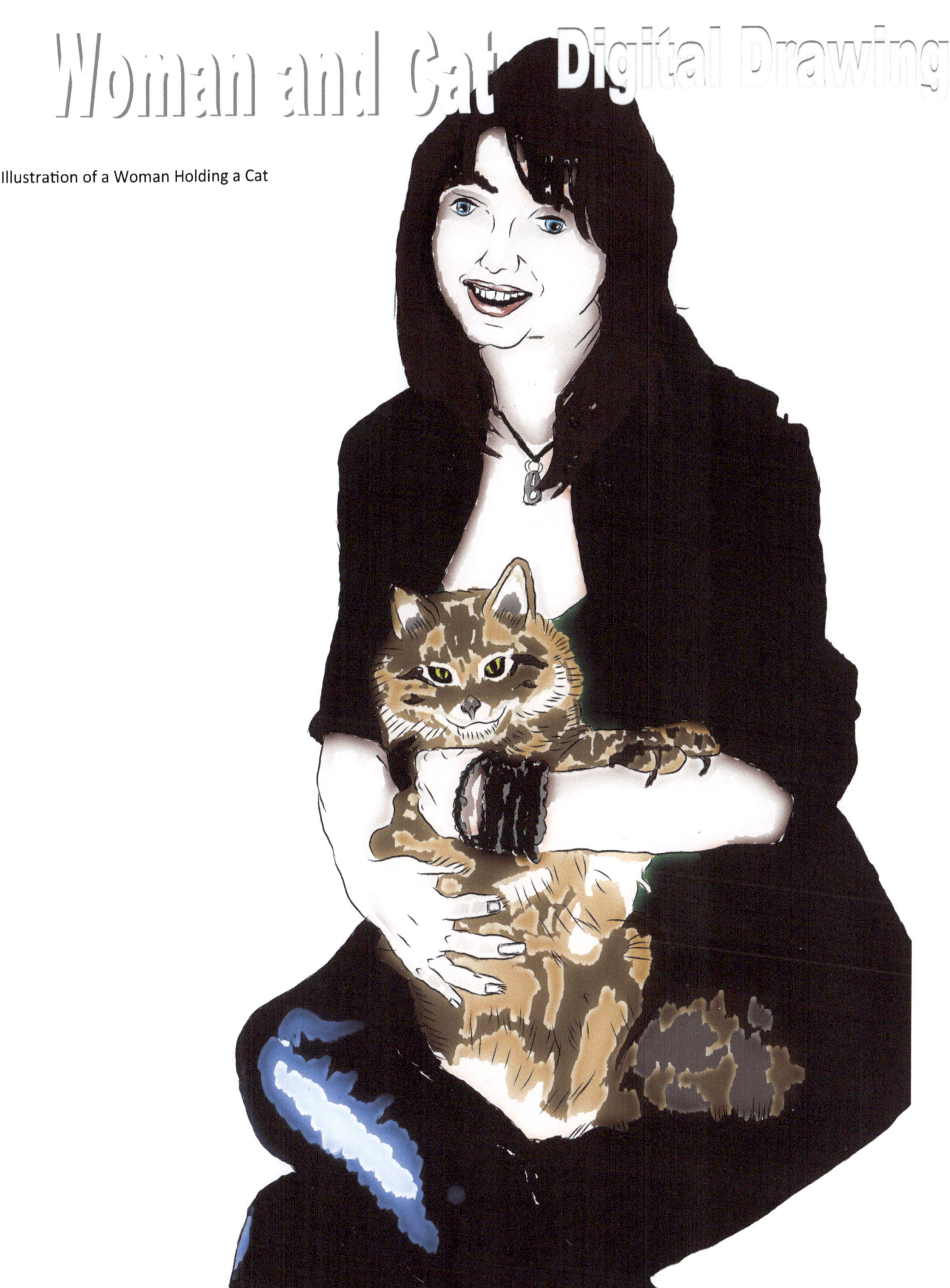

Heathen Art

Benjamin Long

The images contained in this portfolio are the property of Heathen Art or clients of Heathen Art and may not be reproduced, altered in part or whole in any way without permission from Heathen Art, or Benjamin Long. Reproductions of said work in this portfolio are a violation of Title 17 of the United States Revised Code.

If you would like to use an image depicted in this portfolio under the fair use guidelines then contact Heathen Art and you may be provided with a sample or the piece that you request at a lower resolution and size. Contact information is located at the bottom of this page. If the Art in question is property of a client of Heathen Art then the inquiry must be approved by the Client that hired the work and Heathen Art would not be able to give permission for usage of artwork.

Per company rules any art that Heathen art does may be utilized in this portfolio per the agreement for service from heathen art.

Contained are 43 Pieces of art by Artist Benjamin Long, Illustrator for Heathen Art. If you would like to contact Benjamin the follow the contact instructions at the bottom of this page.

http://whitewolfheathen.deviantart.com

Benjamin Long

President, Heathen Art

wiking88142001@yahoo.com

Ebay Store

Ohio Heathen Art

Skype

whitewolfheathen

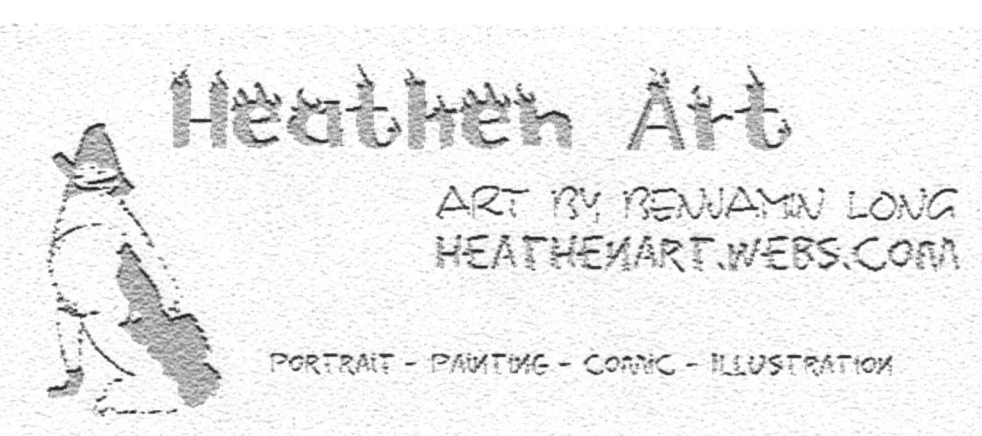

Heathen Art
ART BY BENJAMIN LONG
HEATHENART.WEBS.COM

PORTRAIT - PAINTING - COMIC - ILLUSTRATION

www.ingramcontent.com/pod-product-compliance
Lightning Source LLC
Chambersburg PA
CBHW051109180526
45172CB00002B/843

* 9 7 8 1 4 7 0 1 1 8 0 2 0 *